HABAKKUK

Habakkuk

Sorrowful, Yet Always Rejoicing

ANGELA K. LEE

CONTENTS

~ 7 ~
# By Faith: Sorrowful, Yet Always Rejoicing

A PLAN FOR THIS STUDY

This study is based on the Observation, Interpretation, and Application method of Bible study. Each lesson's questions and commentary help you move through these steps:

Observation: What does the text say?

Read the entire text for comprehension.

Read again and consider: Who was this written to?

What is happening in the passage? When and where did this take place? Why did the author write this?

Mark any keywords, repeated phrases, or ideas.

Notice any lists, contrasts, comparisons, or types of imagery used.

Interpretation: What does the text mean?

Consult different translations.

Look up cross-references and consider: What do other parts of the Bible have to say about these ideas?

What would the original hearers have thought?

How does this passage fit into the larger story of the Bible? (Creation-Fall-Redemption-New Creation) [see page 5]

Paraphrase: Rewrite the text in your own words.

Consult reliable commentaries.

Application: How do I apply it to my life?

What does the passage tell us about God?

What does this passage tell you about your sin and your need for a Savior?

Is there a command to obey? Is there a promise to claim?

How might this truth transform my life, prayers, and perspective today?

Seeing Jesus in Habakkuk

After His resurrection, Jesus instructed how we are to interpret books like Habakkuk.

> "Then he said to them, 'These are my words that I spoke to you while I was still with you, that everything written about me in the Law of Moses and the Prophets and the Psalms must be fulfilled." Then he opened their minds to understand the Scriptures and said to them, 'Thus it is written, that the Christ should suffer and on the third day rise from the dead, and that repentance for the forgiveness of sins should be proclaimed in his name to all nations, beginning from Jerusalem.'" (Luke 24:44-47)

The second *interpretation* section of each lesson moves you through these questions:

Does the New Testament quote or allude to this text? If so, how does the later interpretation shed light on the passage at hand?

Does this text speak directly about Christ?

How do the implications of the Gospel make these commands possible?

Does this text reveal a person, event, or object in the Old Testament that points toward Christ?

Is this passage predictive of Christ?

How does this passage show us humanity's need for Christ?

How does this passage reveal God's redemptive nature?

Does the passage reveal a biblical theme that points to Christ?

Does the passage show a promise of God that points us to Christ?

(Akin, 10)

~ 1 ~

INTRODUCTION TO HABAKKUK

Observation & Interpretation

1. Habakkuk likely lived in the time after Josiah's reign, and before the Babylonian captivity. Read **2 Chronicles 34-36** to learn details of the nation's history that would have shaped Habakkuk's experience. Record your observations below.

34 Josiah was eight years old when he began to reign, and he reigned thirty-one years in Jerusalem. ² And he did what was right in the eyes of the Lord, and walked in the ways of David his father; and he did not turn aside to the right hand or to the left. ³ For in the eighth year of his reign, while he was yet a boy, he began to seek the God of David his father, and in the twelfth year he began to purge Judah and Jerusalem of the high places, the Asherim, and the carved and the metal images. ⁴ And they chopped down the altars of the Baals in his presence, and he cut down the incense altars that stood above them. And he broke in pieces the Asherim and the carved and the metal images, and he made dust of them and scattered it over the graves of those who had sacrificed to them. ⁵ He also burned the bones of the priests on their altars and cleansed

Judah and Jerusalem. ⁶ And in the cities of Manasseh, Ephraim, and Simeon, and as far as Naphtali, in their ruins[a] all around, ⁷ he broke down the altars and beat the Asherim and the images into powder and cut down all the incense altars throughout all the land of Israel. Then he returned to Jerusalem.

⁸ Now in the eighteenth year of his reign, when he had cleansed the land and the house, he sent Shaphan the son of Azaliah, and Maaseiah the governor of the city, and Joah the son of Joahaz, the recorder, to repair the house of the Lord his God. ⁹ They came to Hilkiah the high priest and gave him the money that had been brought into the house of God, which the Levites, the keepers of the threshold, had collected from Manasseh and Ephraim and from all the remnant of Israel and from all Judah and Benjamin and from the inhabitants of Jerusalem. ¹⁰ And they gave it to the workmen who were working in the house of the Lord. And the workmen who were working in the house of the Lord gave it for repairing and restoring the house. ¹¹ They gave it to the carpenters and the builders to buy quarried stone, and timber for binders and beams for the buildings that the kings of Judah had let go to ruin. ¹² And the men did the work faithfully. Over them were set Jahath and Obadiah the Levites, of the sons of Merari, and Zechariah and Meshullam, of the sons of the Kohathites, to have oversight. The Levites, all who were skillful with instruments of music, ¹³ were over the burden-bearers and directed all who did work in every kind of service, and some of the Levites were scribes and officials and gatekeepers.

¹⁴ While they were bringing out the money that had been brought into the house of the Lord, Hilkiah the priest found the Book of the Law of the Lord given through Moses. ¹⁵ Then Hilkiah answered and said to Shaphan the secretary, "I have found the Book of the Law in the house of the Lord." And Hilkiah gave the book to Shaphan. ¹⁶ Shaphan brought the book to the king, and further reported to the king, "All that was committed to your servants they are doing. ¹⁷ They have emptied out the money that was found in the house of

the Lord and have given it into the hand of the overseers and the workmen." [18] Then Shaphan the secretary told the king, "Hilkiah the priest has given me a book." And Shaphan read from it before the king.

[19] And when the king heard the words of the Law, he tore his clothes. [20] And the king commanded Hilkiah, Ahikam the son of Shaphan, Abdon the son of Micah, Shaphan the secretary, and Asaiah the king's servant, saying, [21] "Go, inquire of the Lord for me and for those who are left in Israel and in Judah, concerning the words of the book that has been found. For great is the wrath of the Lord that is poured out on us, because our fathers have not kept the word of the Lord, to do according to all that is written in this book."

[22] So Hilkiah and those whom the king had sent went to Huldah the prophetess, the wife of Shallum the son of Tokhath, son of Hasrah, keeper of the wardrobe (now she lived in Jerusalem in the Second Quarter) and spoke to her to that effect. [23] And she said to them, "Thus says the Lord, the God of Israel: 'Tell the man who sent you to me, [24] Thus says the Lord, Behold, I will bring disaster upon this place and upon its inhabitants, all the curses that are written in the book that was read before the king of Judah. [25] Because they have forsaken me and have made offerings to other gods, that they might provoke me to anger with all the works of their hands, therefore my wrath will be poured out on this place and will not be quenched. [26] But to the king of Judah, who sent you to inquire of the Lord, thus shall you say to him, Thus says the Lord, the God of Israel: Regarding the words that you have heard, [27] because your heart was tender and you humbled yourself before God when you heard his words against this place and its inhabitants, and you have humbled yourself before me and have torn your clothes and wept before me, I also have heard you, declares the Lord. [28] Behold, I will gather you to your fathers, and you shall be gathered to your grave in peace, and your eyes shall not see all the disaster that I will bring

upon this place and its inhabitants.'" And they brought back word to the king.

²⁹ Then the king sent and gathered together all the elders of Judah and Jerusalem. ³⁰ And the king went up to the house of the Lord, with all the men of Judah and the inhabitants of Jerusalem and the priests and the Levites, all the people both great and small. And he read in their hearing all the words of the Book of the Covenant that had been found in the house of the Lord. ³¹ And the king stood in his place and made a covenant before the Lord, to walk after the Lord and to keep his commandments and his testimonies and his statutes, with all his heart and all his soul, to perform the words of the covenant that were written in this book. ³² Then he made all who were present in Jerusalem and in Benjamin join in it. And the inhabitants of Jerusalem did according to the covenant of God, the God of their fathers. ³³ And Josiah took away all the abominations from all the territory that belonged to the people of Israel and made all who were present in Israel serve the Lord their God. All his days they did not turn away from following the Lord, the God of their fathers.

35 Josiah kept a Passover to the Lord in Jerusalem. And they slaughtered the Passover lamb on the fourteenth day of the first month. ² He appointed the priests to their offices and encouraged them in the service of the house of the Lord. ³ And he said to the Levites who taught all Israel and who were holy to the Lord, "Put the holy ark in the house that Solomon the son of David, king of Israel, built. You need not carry it on your shoulders. Now serve the Lord your God and his people Israel. ⁴ Prepare yourselves according to your fathers' houses by your divisions, as prescribed in the writing of David king of Israel and the document of Solomon his son. ⁵ And stand in the Holy Place according to the groupings of the fathers' houses of your brothers the lay people, and according to the division of the Levites by fathers' household. ⁶ And slaughter

the Passover lamb, and consecrate yourselves, and prepare for your brothers, to do according to the word of the Lord by[a] Moses."

[7] Then Josiah contributed to the lay people, as Passover offerings for all who were present, lambs and young goats from the flock to the number of 30,000, and 3,000 bulls; these were from the king's possessions. [8] And his officials contributed willingly to the people, to the priests, and to the Levites. Hilkiah, Zechariah, and Jehiel, the chief officers of the house of God, gave to the priests for the Passover offerings 2,600 Passover lambs and 300 bulls. [9] Conaniah also, and Shemaiah and Nethanel his brothers, and Hashabiah and Jeiel and Jozabad, the chiefs of the Levites, gave to the Levites for the Passover offerings 5,000 lambs and young goats and 500 bulls.

[10] When the service had been prepared for, the priests stood in their place, and the Levites in their divisions according to the king's command. [11] And they slaughtered the Passover lamb, and the priests threw the blood that they received from them while the Levites flayed the sacrifices. [12] And they set aside the burnt offerings that they might distribute them according to the groupings of the fathers' houses of the lay people, to offer to the Lord, as it is written in the Book of Moses. And so they did with the bulls. [13] And they roasted the Passover lamb with fire according to the rule; and they boiled the holy offerings in pots, in cauldrons, and in pans, and carried them quickly to all the lay people. [14] And afterward they prepared for themselves and for the priests, because the priests, the sons of Aaron, were offering the burnt offerings and the fat parts until night; so the Levites prepared for themselves and for the priests, the sons of Aaron. [15] The singers, the sons of Asaph, were in their place according to the command of David, and Asaph, and Heman, and Jeduthun the king's seer; and the gatekeepers were at each gate. They did not need to depart from their service, for their brothers the Levites prepared for them.

[16] So all the service of the Lord was prepared that day, to keep the Passover and to offer burnt offerings on the altar of the Lord, according to the command of King Josiah. [17] And the people of Israel

who were present kept the Passover at that time, and the Feast of Unleavened Bread seven days. ¹⁸ No Passover like it had been kept in Israel since the days of Samuel the prophet. None of the kings of Israel had kept such a Passover as was kept by Josiah, and the priests and the Levites, and all Judah and Israel who were present, and the inhabitants of Jerusalem. ¹⁹ In the eighteenth year of the reign of Josiah this Passover was kept.

²⁰ After all this, when Josiah had prepared the temple, Neco king of Egypt went up to fight at Carchemish on the Euphrates, and Josiah went out to meet him. ²¹ But he sent envoys to him, saying, "What have we to do with each other, king of Judah? I am not coming against you this day, but against the house with which I am at war. And God has commanded me to hurry. Cease opposing God, who is with me, lest he destroy you." ²² Nevertheless, Josiah did not turn away from him, but disguised himself in order to fight with him. He did not listen to the words of Neco from the mouth of God, but came to fight in the plain of Megiddo. ²³ And the archers shot King Josiah. And the king said to his servants, "Take me away, for I am badly wounded." ²⁴ So his servants took him out of the chariot and carried him in his second chariot and brought him to Jerusalem. And he died and was buried in the tombs of his fathers. All Judah and Jerusalem mourned for Josiah. ²⁵ Jeremiah also uttered a lament for Josiah; and all the singing men and singing women have spoken of Josiah in their laments to this day. They made these a rule in Israel; behold, they are written in the Laments. ²⁶ Now the rest of the acts of Josiah, and his good deeds according to what is written in the Law of the Lord, ²⁷ and his acts, first and last, behold, they are written in the Book of the Kings of Israel and Judah.

36 The people of the land took Jehoahaz the son of Josiah and made him king in his father's place in Jerusalem. ² Jehoahaz was twenty-three years old when he began to reign, and he reigned three months in Jerusalem. ³ Then the king of Egypt deposed him in Jerusalem and laid on the land a tribute of a hundred talents of

silver and a talent of gold. ⁴And the king of Egypt made Eliakim his brother king over Judah and Jerusalem, and changed his name to Jehoiakim. But Neco took Jehoahaz his brother and carried him to Egypt.

⁵Jehoiakim was twenty-five years old when he began to reign, and he reigned eleven years in Jerusalem. He did what was evil in the sight of the Lord his God.⁶Against him came up Nebuchad-nezzar king of Babylon and bound him in chains to take him to Babylon. ⁷Nebuchadnezzar also carried part of the vessels of the house of the Lord to Babylon and put them in his palace in Babylon. ⁸Now the rest of the acts of Jehoiakim, and the abominations that he did, and what was found against him, behold, they are written in the Book of the Kings of Israel and Judah. And Jehoiachin his son reigned in his place.

⁹Jehoiachin was eighteen years old when he became king, and he reigned three months and ten days in Jerusalem. He did what was evil in the sight of the Lord.¹⁰In the spring of the year King Neb-uchadnezzar sent and brought him to Babylon, with the precious vessels of the house of the Lord, and made his brother Zedekiah king over Judah and Jerusalem.

¹¹Zedekiah was twenty-one years old when he began to reign, and he reigned eleven years in Jerusalem. ¹²He did what was evil in the sight of the Lord his God. He did not humble himself before Jeremiah the prophet, who spoke from the mouth of the Lord. ¹³He also rebelled against King Nebuchadnezzar, who had made him swear by God. He stiffened his neck and hardened his heart against turning to the Lord, the God of Israel. ¹⁴All the officers of the priests and the people likewise were exceedingly unfaithful, following all the abominations of the nations. And they polluted the house of the Lord that he had made holy in Jerusalem.

¹⁵The Lord, the God of their fathers, sent persistently to them by his messengers, because he had compassion on his people and on his dwelling place. ¹⁶But they kept mocking the messengers of God,

despising his words and scoffing at his prophets, until the wrath of the Lord rose against his people, until there was no remedy.

¹⁷ Therefore he brought up against them the king of the Chaldeans, who killed their young men with the sword in the house of their sanctuary and had no compassion on young man or virgin, old man or aged. He gave them all into his hand. ¹⁸ And all the vessels of the house of God, great and small, and the treasures of the house of the Lord, and the treasures of the king and of his princes, all these he brought to Babylon. ¹⁹ And they burned the house of God and broke down the wall of Jerusalem and burned all its palaces with fire and destroyed all its precious vessels. ²⁰ He took into exile in Babylon those who had escaped from the sword, and they became servants to him and to his sons until the establishment of the kingdom of Persia, ²¹ to fulfill the word of the Lord by the mouth of Jeremiah, until the land had enjoyed its Sabbaths. All the days that it lay desolate it kept Sabbath, to fulfill seventy years.

²² Now in the first year of Cyrus king of Persia, that the word of the Lord by the mouth of Jeremiah might be fulfilled, the Lord stirred up the spirit of Cyrus king of Persia, so that he made a proclamation throughout all his kingdom and also put it in writing: ²³ "Thus says Cyrus king of Persia, 'The Lord, the God of heaven, has given me all the kingdoms of the earth, and he has charged me to build him a house at Jerusalem, which is in Judah. Whoever is among you of all his people, may the Lord his God be with him. Let him go up.'"

Read Habakkuk 1:1 and consider the following questions.

1 The oracle that Habakkuk the prophet saw.

2. Read the following different translations of **Habakkuk 1:1**.

ESV The oracle that Habakkuk the prophet saw.

NIV The prophecy that Habakkuk the prophet received.

CSB The pronouncement that the prophet Habakkuk saw.

NKJV The burden which the prophet Habakkuk saw.

NLT This is the message that the prophet Habakkuk received in a vision.

What do the different words tell you about the intended meaning of this verse?

3. Verse 1 is a superscription — like the address of a letter. What does this verse tell you about the book of Habakkuk?

Commentary

Background of Habakkuk

Who wrote Habakkuk?

Habakkuk was written by the prophet Habakkuk. He was likely a contemporary of Zephaniah and Jeremiah, and he was a prophet to the nation of Judah.

When was Habakkuk written?

The specific time period Habakkuk wrote is unknown, but it was probably near the end of Josiah's reign (640-609 B.C.). Most scholars agree Habakkuk's time frame was after the invasion of Nineveh in 612 B.C, but before the Babylonian exile in 587 B.C (ESV Study Bible).

Where does Habakkuk fit in with the whole story of the Bible?

God has spoken to His people since Genesis. He spoke creation into being, and He had a plan to bless the world with His grace and glory. After the fall, which separated humanity from God (Genesis 3), God promised to rescue his people and dwell with them again. He continued speaking through men He appointed like Noah and Abraham, and God made a covenant with Abraham to bless his family, make them a nation, and provide a place for them (Genesis 12). Abraham's family became the Hebrew nation of Israel. Through many trials and wanderings, including enslavement in Egypt (Exodus 1), God was faithful to keep His covenant and rescue His people. He used Moses to deliver Israel from Egypt, and this deliverance became a marker to help them remember God's salvation and point them to a greater deliverance to come. Building on the covenant he had made with Abraham, God made the Mosaic covenant with Israel, promising them relationship with Him as a nation of priests, and He gave them His law at Mount Sinai to show them how to live faithfully to Him. But, the Israelites' sinful state made it so they couldn't dwell with God or hear His words without mediators. So, through Moses, the law and sacrificial system were put in place, and God clarified the ramifications of His covenant by promising blessings for obedience and warning them of curses for disobedience. The blessings included protection and fruitfulness in their promised land, and the curses included barrenness, suffering, and deportation from the land God had given them. When Israel sinned, priests were called to intercede for the people (Deuteronomy 27-28, Exodus 19-31).

Later on, God appointed judges to guide them, and at the request of Israel, kings ruled over them (I Samuel 8). These judges and kings were to keep God's law, but instead, they often led the people astray. So, God continued to raise up **prophets** who were to **speak** to His people on His behalf. The prophets were to remind Israel of God's covenant with them.

In Habakkuk's day, God's people were divided into two kingdoms: Israel in the North and Judah in the South. **Habakkuk was a prophet in Judah.** He was of the generation after the prophets Jeremiah and Ezekiel, and he would have been a contemporary of theirs. As a prophet, Habakkuk's job was to stand in between God and man to testify about the truth of God to the world. Prophets spoke of God's promises, commanded repentance, warned of judgement, and foretold future events—often about God's judgement for sin.

Because of the wicked leadership of Judah's kings, the nation was morally and spiritually corrupt. Judah would have been aware of God's covenant promises to keep them (Genesis 12), their obligation to obey the law (Exodus 20, Deuteronomy 27-28), and God's promise to restore them if they repented of their sin (Deuteronomy 30:1-10).

Even with all this knowledge and all of this hope, God's people were rejecting Him and refused to repent. However, Habakkuk would have witnessed a brief revival under King Josiah. In 2 Chronicles 24-26, we read about Josiah's righteous reforms. Under his reign, God's people returned to God through His word, the sacrificial system, and the sacraments. Habakkuk's experience of the power of God's word sparking revival among His people may have contributed to the prophet's longing to see God's righteousness again.

As Habakkuk watched the ebbs and flows of his nation's spiritual and economic livelihood, the surrounding empires were also rising and falling in strength. Assyria had ruled the northern kingdom of Israel for 100 years, but they were weakening, and Babylon was becoming more powerful. It was a weary and difficult political climate with rumors of wars and exile on the horizon. O. Palmer Robertson explains, "In an era when mighty nations clash, the divine response comes in the form of words from men unknown among the nations of the world. Mightier than human armies is the prophetic word of God" (Robertson,1990, p. 38). During this chaotic time, Habakkuk's purpose was to reveal this "divine response," and speak truth to God's people on His behalf.

Habakkuk probably lived to see: the destruction of Nineveh by Babylon in 612 B.C, the battle of Haran in 609 B.C. when Josiah died, the final defeat of the Assyrians at the battle of Carchemish, and the fulfillment of his own prophecy of the Babylonian invasion of Judah (ESV Study Bible).

Commentary on Habakkuk 1:1

Verse 1: The book starts with a superscription, which serves as an address or label for the entire book. It explains that the book of Habakkuk is...

"The oracle..."

An oracle is a word that means a burden, tribute, prophecy, or utterance. It refers to God's word to man, and in prophetic literature, it usually referred to God's message to a prophet (Fentress, 2018, p.181). In Isaiah, "oracle" is used as a substitute for "burden" (Isaiah 31:1). The message prophets received would feel like a heavy burden to them until they shared it. Habakkuk's message, of the destruction of his own people and land, was certainly a weight on his shoulders.

that Habakkuk the prophet....

Myths and legends have attempted to fill out the story of Habakkuk's life and character, but other prophets don't mention him. We are simply told he is a prophet of God. Habakkuk's message was significant, not because of who he was, but because he was "a voice crying out in the wilderness..." (Isaiah 40:3, John 1:23) to tell others about God's judgement and mercy.

Saw..."

It is not clear whether Habakkuk saw a vision from God, or if the word "saw" just refers to the fact that Habakkuk received a divine prophecy from outside himself. Ken Fentress explained, "the words *hearing* and *seeing* are the language of divine revelation, and they reflect the language of understanding" (Fentress, 2018, p. 183). However the oracle came, Habakkuk had received and understood a message from God. What follows is the story of the ways he came to understand it, his conversation with God, and the work of God that transformed Habakkuk's heart and faith.

A Summary of Habakkuk

Habakkuk is a prophetic book that is a conversation between the prophet and God. When Habakkuk faces questions about God's justice and will, he turns to the Lord. When we read Habakkuk, the book gives us insight into Habakkuk's vision, and we get to see the ways God worked in him to change his heart and lead him to worship.

The first two chapters contain Habakkuk's prayer and complaint, and the Lord's replies. This book has all the elements of a Biblical lament- or an expression of deep grief, regret, or sorrow. Habakkuk grieves and complains about the spiritual and moral deterioration around him. God responds by telling him He would execute justice on Judah, and He would do it through the wicked nation of Babylon. When Habakkuk understands that a nation as wicked as Babylon would conquer his own nation, it troubles him even more. So, Habakkuk cried out again, and God responds to this lament by reassuring him that He would save Judah, and judge Babylon for their wicked acts, too. And though Habakkuk didn't fully understand God's ways, as he reflected on God's power of salvation in Israel's past, he learned to trust Him by the end of the book (ESV Study Bible).

What is the literary genre and style of Habakkuk?

Habakkuk is a Minor prophet; the term "minor" refers to the length of the book compared to other prophetic books.

The literary style of Habakkuk is a dialogue; it is a question-and-answer session between Habakkuk and God. There are also poetic elements like imagery throughout the book.

An outline tells us more:

1:2-11

Habakkuk's Lament

God's response

1:12-2:20

Habakkuk's Lament

God's response

3:1-19

Habakkuk's Prayer

The book concludes with a full psalm, a prayer of praise to God that was formalized for corporate worship. (Habakkuk 3:19)

Themes of this Study

Seeing Jesus Christ in Habakkuk

After His resurrection, Jesus taught the disciples how to interpret books like Habakkuk.

"Then he said to them, 'These are my words that I spoke to you while I was still with you, that everything written about me in the Law of Moses and the Prophets and the Psalms must be fulfilled.' Then he opened their minds to understand the Scriptures and said to them, 'Thus it is written, that the Christ should suffer and on the third day rise from the dead, and that repentance for the forgiveness of sins should be proclaimed in his name to all nations, beginning from Jerusalem'" (Luke 24:44-47).

Jesus fulfills all of scripture, including the prophets. Habakkuk is a book about an imperfect prophet who longed for God's justice and leaves us yearning for our true, Just Prophet. Jesus not only perfectly lamented over the sin of His people, but bore God's justice for them on the cross. In Habakkuk's prayer, he experienced both grief and joy—and Jesus secured for His people a path from grief to eternal joy in Himself. Each week, the second interpretation lesson of each chapter will help us understand how we see Jesus in the book of Habakkuk. (There is an additional list of interpretation questions in *A Plan for This Study* for reference.) Jesus is the true and better Habakkuk through His life, death, and resurrection.

The Practice of Biblical Lament

Habakkuk has all the elements of a Biblical Lament. Author Mark Vroegop defines lament as "a prayer in pain that leads to trust" (Vroegop, 2019, p. 38), and he outlines the process of Biblical Lament with these steps:

1. **Turn to God**
2. **Bring your Complaint**
3. **Ask Boldly**
4. **Choose to Trust**

Habakkuk grieves over the widespread suffering and sin of Judah, and he also grieves over the personal implications this suffering has for his own life (Habakkuk 3:16-19). As a prophet, Habakkuk studied God's heart, and he would have been intimately aware of what broke God's heart. With this spiritual training to guide him, when Habakkuk saw that his homeland, Judah, was filled with the pain of sin and suffering, his response was to cry out to God in lament. His honest prayer allowed him to fully grieve, and it simultaneously led him to a deep trust in the mercy, justice, and sovereignty of the God of salvation.

In this study, we will explore Habakkuk's lament, and consider how we might carry out this practice in our own prayer life.

Living by Faith in the God of Our Salvation

As God instructs Habakkuk on how to live in the tension between grief and hope, He tells him in Habakkuk 2:4, "the righteous shall live by his faith."

Old Testament prophets like Habakkuk modeled living by faith. As the writer of Hebrews says, though they could not see the full reward, they responded to the turmoil they faced by welcoming the promises of our salvation from afar. (Hebrews 11:13). Robertson eloquently explains, "A matured faith trusts humbly but persistently in God's design for establishing righteousness in the earth" (Robertson, 1990, p. 136). Walking by faith is an underlying theme throughout Habakkuk. When Habakkuk suffered, God encouraged him to live by faith in the God of Salvation.

Paul has quoted Habakkuk 2:4 in New Testament, most famously in Romans 1:16-17. Christians are to respond to the life, death, and resurrection of Christ *by faith* in Him. We live *by faith* in the cross— our proof that even when our suffering and painful circumstances make no earthly sense, God is for us. We are to respond to questions about living in our fallen world *by faith* in the One who loved us, who gave Himself for us, and who is coming soon to restore all things.

What does it mean to do this? How do we walk by faith in the God of Salvation through perplexing circumstances and suffering? What does it mean on this side of the cross? These are questions and practices we will explore as we study Habakkuk's prayer and prophecy.

Application & Reflection

1. Habakkuk had impressionable knowledge and memories of God's reviving word and justice. It made his heart break over the injustice and corruption he saw. Recall a time when you saw the power of God's word and justice. What did you learn about God?

2. How does this knowledge of a just and powerful God inform your view of the brokenness and injustice that you see?

How might this inform your prayer life?

3. What do you want to learn from Habakkuk about the practice of biblical lament?

~ 2 ~

BY FAITH: POUR OUT YOUR HEART

Observation & Interpretation

Habakkuk 1:1-11

Read Habakkuk 1:1-11 and consider the following questions.

1 The oracle that Habakkuk the prophet saw.
2 O Lord, how long shall I cry for help,
    and you will not hear?
Or cry to you "Violence!"
    and you will not save?
3 Why do you make me see iniquity,
    and why do you idly look at wrong?
Destruction and violence are before me;
    strife and contention arise.
4 So the law is paralyzed,
    and justice never goes forth.
For the wicked surround the righteous;
    so justice goes forth perverted.

5 "Look among the nations, and see;
    wonder and be astounded.

For I am doing a work in your days
   that you would not believe if told.
6 For behold, I am raising up the Chaldeans,
   that bitter and hasty nation,
who march through the breadth of the earth,
   to seize dwellings not their own.
7 They are dreaded and fearsome;
   their justice and dignity go forth from themselves.
8 Their horses are swifter than leopards,
   more fierce than the evening wolves;
   their horsemen press proudly on.
Their horsemen come from afar;
   they fly like an eagle swift to devour.
9 They all come for violence,
   all their faces forward.
   They gather captives like sand.
10 At kings they scoff,
   and at rulers they laugh.
They laugh at every fortress,
   for they pile up earth and take it.
11 Then they sweep by like the wind and go on,
   guilty men, whose own might is their god!"

1. We may break these verses up into 2 sections. Verses 2-4 are Habakkuk's prayer and 5-11 are God's answer.

Read verses 2-4 and list any repeated phrases or ideas that stand out to you in Habakkuk's complaint.

2. What does Habakkuk's language make you think about his relationship with God?

3. Judah's condition during this period is also described in **Jeremiah 9:2-6, Micah 7:3,** and **Isaiah 59:4.** How do these additional verses give insight into Judah's spiritual and moral state?

²Oh that I had in the desert
   a travelers' lodging place,
that I might leave my people
   and go away from them!
For they are all adulterers,
   a company of treacherous men.
³They bend their tongue like a bow;
   falsehood and not truth has grown strong[c] in the land;
for they proceed from evil to evil,
   and they do not know me, declares the Lord.
   ⁴Let everyone beware of his neighbor,
   and put no trust in any brother,
for every brother is a deceiver,
   and every neighbor goes about as a slanderer.
⁵Everyone deceives his neighbor,
   and no one speaks the truth;
they have taught their tongue to speak lies;
   they weary themselves committing iniquity.
⁶Heaping oppression upon oppression, and deceit upon deceit,
   they refuse to know me, declares the Lord.

³Their hands are on what is evil, to do it well;

the prince and the judge ask for a bribe,
and the great man utters the evil desire of his soul;
    thus they weave it together.

⁴ No one enters suit justly;
    no one goes to law honestly;
they rely on empty pleas, they speak lies,
    they conceive mischief and give birth to iniquity.

4. Considering verse 4, what effect was corruption having on God's law "going forth"?

Why do you think this was painful for Habakkuk?

Commentary

Verses 2-3

As Habakkuk opens, we learn he is a man of prayer. This is a personal, one-on-one conversation between Habakkuk and God. Habakkuk was speaking about Judah; a corrupt and suffering nation surrounded him, so he turned to his Lord.

He says, "O Lord, how long shall I cry for help and you will not hear?" This first phrase tells us that Habakkuk had been crying out to God for a long time without a response. He echoed cries of the anguished psalmist's pleas of "How long..." and he relied on their example as he prayed. Throughout Israel's history, God also cried out "How long..." as He expressed His pain over Israel's rebellion in Exodus 16:28 and Numbers 14:11 (Robertson, 1990, p.138). Habakkuk knew God experienced a longing grief over His people's sin, so he took refuge in God's heart as he cried out in lament.

Verses 2 and 3 continue and say, "Or cry to you "Violence!" and you will not save?" Other prophets like Ezekiel and Jeremiah give more insight into Judah's violence—God's people had rejected him, and they were full of deceit and corruption. The righteousness and flourishing that came with Josiah's reforms were a powerful but distant memory, and idol worship, sin, and injustice were rampant. Habakkuk waited for God to "save," and he had received no answer.

Habakkuk's next cry was "Why..." He was confused about why he had to watch Judah's spiritual and moral decline and witness God's apparent idleness at the same time. This is the cry of a weary prophet who longed for God's justice and righteousness.

Verse 4

In verse 4, Habakkuk described the effect sin had on the justice system. The "law" could be referring to the Torah (God's law) or the law of the state—but because Habakkuk is speaking about God's people, it's likely he is talking about *God's law*. The spiritual state of Judah caused God's word to be "paralyzed," numb, and ineffective. Nobody received justice because they were hemmed in by wicked leadership that twisted the scriptures for their selfish purposes. The truth, protection, and blessing that came with God's holy law could not "go forth."

Observation and Interpretation (Contd.)

1. What are God's instructions for Habakkuk in verse 5?

2. Verses 5-11 reveal that God had already been working to answer Habakkuk's cry for justice. What was God preparing to do?

3. God continues and describes the Babylonian war machine. List some phrases about Babylon that stand out to you from verses 6-11.

4. As a part of God's covenant with Israel, He declared a list of blessings and curses through Moses. If Israel obeyed and kept their covenant, they would experience blessings; if they disobeyed and failed to keep their covenant, they would experience curses. Read **Deuteronomy 28:25, 36.** How was God raising up Babylon an example of Him keeping His word and covenant?

25 "The Lord will cause you to be defeated before your enemies. You shall go out one way against them and flee seven ways before them. And you shall be a horror to all the kingdoms of the earth.

36 "The Lord will bring you and your king whom you set over you to a nation that neither you nor your fathers have known. And there you shall serve other gods of wood and stone.

Commentary

As God responded to Habakkuk, He revealed He had already been working to answer Habakkuk's prayer. God does not correct him or minimize his concerns over the state of Judah. Instead, when it came to Judah's corruption, God's heart was even more broken than Habakkuk's. God had a plan so stunning and powerful that He began His answer with a warning; Habakkuk was told to brace himself for the incredible act of judgement he was about to see.

Verses 5-6

God answers Habakkuk by telling him to "look among the nations and see..." Habakkuk thought he had already "looked" and "seen," (Habakkuk 1:3) but God is the one who truly sees all things, and He was telling Habakkuk to look again. What God was about to do would proclaim His glory over all the earth, and His acts would be worthy of "wonder." God was going to do this work "in [their] days..." meaning, God's answer was going to come in the lifetime of Habakkuk and his contemporaries. This phrase "in your days" is one that scholars used to date the writing of the book of Habakkuk; God was giving Habakkuk a prophecy that he would live to see during his own life. The Lord warned His announcement was so shocking that Habakkuk would hardly believe it.

Why? God was going to "raise up the Chaldeans." "The Chaldeans" is another term for the Babylonians. They were an ethnically diverse Aramean tribe in Southern Babylon that started to gain strength and power as Assyria weakened (ESV Study Bible). Historical research helps us understand that the speed with which this tribe rose to power was indeed supernatural, and "God rose them up." Robertson tells us that "they became the world rulers over Babylonia, Assyria, Palestine, and Egypt, when twenty years previously they were hardly known to exist" (Roberston, 1990, p.149). God's work among the nations is a wonder. He orders the rise and fall of empires according to His purpose and for His glory.

God was raising up the Babylonians, and they were coming to conquer Israel and devastate the nation. This judgement would be horrible, but God was not acting out of rash impulse as he disciplined His people. The conditions of God's covenant agreement with Israel laid out this exact punishment for them. In Deuteronomy 27 and 28, Moses called Israel to hear the blessings of obedience and curses of disobedience that came with their position as God's chosen people. God held out promises of abundant life, prosperity, and blessings for when Israel faithfully obeyed God's words. But if they disobeyed His commandments, curses would come and "overtake them." In Deuteronomy 28:25-44, we see the terrifying curse of Israel being "defeated before their enemies" and being "given to nations" they did not know. Habakkuk's assessment of Judah's condition was accurate; they had violently broken their covenant with God and were refusing to repent. So, God kept his word and sent the Chaldeans.

They would attack in a nature that was hostile, "bitter and hasty," and take the land that God once gave to Judah. The Babylonians had the strength and military prowess to take whatever they wanted to from Judah; they would march to take the "dwellings that were not their own."

Verses 7-9

The next verses detail the nature of this judgement as they describe the Babylonian war machine. Judah had been full of violence because of their rebellion against God's law, but Babylon's 'dreadful and fearful' nature stemmed from the fact that they had no sense of law or justice at all—they viewed themselves as their own authority. Their drive came from their worship of themselves.

Their horses were "swifter than leopards." Whatever consolation Israel might have clung to regarding Babylon's physical distance from them would prove empty. Even though they "came from afar", Babylon was fast—they could be there quickly and so danger was imminent. The curses of the covenant had warned them; Habakkuk 1:7 points us to Deuteronomy 28:49, which says, "the Lord will bring a nation against you from far away, from the end of the earth, swooping down like an eagle..."

Babylon's aim was violence. They were focused, forward-facing, and ready to gather captives. Commentators have noted that God used the imagery of sand in His promise to Abraham in Genesis 22:17: "I will surely bless you, and I will surely multiply your offspring as the stars of heaven and as the sand that is on the seashore..." God's people had once seen the picture of sand on the seashore as a reminder of God's blessing. But an army was coming to threaten this blessing. They would gather Israel as "captives like sand."

Verses 10-11

Judah had a dark history of depending on earthly kings for their rescue, but Babylon had such great strength that they responded to all other kings and authorities with prideful laughter. Every barrier, boundary, or fortress that formed against Babylon was just a joke to them, "they laugh." They would simply sweep by "like the wind" and keep moving through to conquer the land that was not theirs. God acknowledges in verse 11 that they are guilty, they see themselves as gods, and they only serve themselves and their own strength.

Interpretation: Seeing Jesus Christ in Habakkuk

1. In His time on earth, Jesus offered lament regarding the corruption of Israel. Read **Matthew 23:13-15, 23-27**. How does Habakkuk's heart for justice in Verses 1-4 point us to Jesus' heart for justice?

[13] "But woe to you, scribes and Pharisees, hypocrites! For you shut the kingdom of heaven in people's faces. For you neither enter yourselves nor allow those who would enter to go in. [15] Woe to you, scribes and Pharisees, hypocrites! For you travel across sea and land to make a single proselyte, and when he becomes a proselyte, you make him twice as much a child of hell as yourselves.

[23] "Woe to you, scribes and Pharisees, hypocrites! For you tithe mint and dill and cumin, and have neglected the weightier matters of the law: justice and mercy and faithfulness. These you ought to have done, without neglecting the others. [24] You blind guides, straining out a gnat and swallowing a camel!

[25] "Woe to you, scribes and Pharisees, hypocrites! For you clean the outside of the cup and the plate, but inside they are full of greed and self-indulgence. [26] You blind Pharisee! First clean the inside of the cup and the plate, that the outside also may be clean.

[27] "Woe to you, scribes and Pharisees, hypocrites! For you are like whitewashed tombs, which outwardly appear beautiful, but within are full of dead people's bones and all uncleanness. [28] So you also outwardly appear righteous to others, but within you are full of hypocrisy and lawlessness.

2. As Jesus lamented over Jerusalem's disobedience, He would have been aware of his obligation to bear God's justice for that disobedience. Read **Galatians 3:10-14**.

¹⁰ For all who rely on works of the law are under a curse; for it is written, "Cursed be everyone who does not abide by all things written in the Book of the Law, and do them." ¹¹ Now it is evident that no one is justified before God by the law, for "The righteous shall live by faith." ¹² But the law is not of faith, rather "The one who does them shall live by them." ¹³ Christ redeemed us from the curse of the law by becoming a curse for us—for it is written, "Cursed is everyone who is hanged on a tree"— ¹⁴ so that in Christ Jesus the blessing of Abraham might come to the Gentiles, so that we might receive the promised Spirit through faith.

How does Jesus relate to the "blessings and curses" of the covenant?

3. We know that Habakkuk's prophecy was fulfilled in part when Babylon came, but Paul quotes Habakkuk 1:5 in Acts 13 and shows us another layer of God's justice. Read **Acts 13:38-41** and **Acts 2:36-41**. What event does Paul imply Habakkuk's prophecy points to?

³⁸ Let it be known to you therefore, brothers, that through this man forgiveness of sins is proclaimed to you, ³⁹ and by him everyone who believes is freed from everything from which you could not be freed by the law of Moses. ⁴⁰ Beware, therefore, lest what is said in the Prophets should come about:
⁴¹ "'Look, you scoffers,
be astounded and perish;

for I am doing a work in your days,
    a work that you will not believe, even if one tells it to you.'"

[36] Let all the house of Israel therefore know for certain that God has made him both Lord and Christ, this Jesus whom you crucified."

[37] Now when they heard this they were cut to the heart, and said to Peter and the rest of the apostles, "Brothers, what shall we do?" [38] And Peter said to them, "Repent and be baptized every one of you in the name of Jesus Christ for the forgiveness of your sins, and you will receive the gift of the Holy Spirit. [39] For the promise is for you and for your children and for all who are far off, everyone whom the Lord our God calls to himself." [40] And with many other words he bore witness and continued to exhort them, saying, "Save yourselves from this crooked generation." [41] So those who received his word were baptized, and there were added that day about three thousand souls.

Prayer & Journaling Prompt

Take some time to thank and praise Jesus that He is...

The *Better* Habakkuk, who perfectly and wholly longs for justice and redemption for His people and achieved this same justice and redemption through His work on the cross.

The Hope of Salvation for covenant breakers through His bearing sin's curse "on a tree."

The One who bore sin's penalty on our behalf, so that through repentance, we might be saved from judgement and experience the joy of knowing God.

Application & Reflection

1. Habakkuk's response to grief over injustice was to *turn to God* in prayer. What is your reaction to our **freedom** to turn to God in our grief?

2. How does the **responsibility** to turn to God in our grief challenge you?

3. Habakkuk echoes the cries of the Psalmists in his lament toward God. How might you use God's word to guide you when you don't know what to pray?

4. When Paul quoted Habakkuk, he called people to **repentance** as he taught Habakkuk 1:5. How might this be an appropriate application for us as we consider God's justice?

5. Habakkuk cried out "How long..." and God's response revealed that He had been seeing and working to answer Habakkuk's cries longer than Habakkuk knew. What does this reveal to you about God's character?

How might this comfort you during times it seems like God is idle?

~ 3 ~

BY FAITH: SURRENDER

Observation & Interpretation
Habakkuk 1:12-2:1

Read **Habakkuk 1:12-2:1** and consider the following questions.

¹² Are you not from everlasting,
O Lord my God, my Holy One?
   We shall not die.
O Lord, you have ordained them as a judgment,
  and you, O Rock, have established them for reproof.
¹³ You who are of purer eyes than to see evil
  and cannot look at wrong,
why do you idly look at traitors
  and remain silent when the wicked swallows up
  the man more righteous than he?
¹⁴ You make mankind like the fish of the sea,
  like crawling things that have no ruler.
¹⁵ He brings all of them up with a hook;
  he drags them out with his net;
he gathers them in his dragnet;
  so he rejoices and is glad.

¹⁶ Therefore he sacrifices to his net
  and makes offerings to his dragnet;
for by them he lives in luxury,
  and his food is rich.
¹⁷ Is he then to keep on emptying his net
  and mercilessly killing nations forever?
   2 I will take my stand at my watchpost
  and station myself on the tower,
and look out to see what he will say to me,
  and what I will answer concerning my complaint.

1. Verse 11 concludes God's description of the ways He will use Babylon to judge Judah, and Verse 12 begins Habakkuk's initial response. Read verse 12; record Habakkuk's response, and what he concludes by the end of the verse.

2. Habakkuk acknowledged God's plan to use Babylon to judge Israel, but he had some more questions. What attributes of God does Habakkuk mention in verses 12-13?

Why do you think he mentions these?

What is his complaint in verse 13?

3. Habakkuk uses imagery from deep sea fishing to describe Babylon's cruel treatment of other nations. Read verses **14-17** in the following translations.

CSB:

[14] You have made mankind
like the fish of the sea,
like marine creatures that have no ruler.
[15] The Chaldeans pull them all up with a hook,
catch them in their dragnet,
and gather them in their fishing net;
that is why they are glad and rejoice.
[16] That is why they sacrifice to their dragnet
and burn incense to their fishing net,
for by these things their portion is rich
and their food plentiful.
[17] Will they therefore empty their net
and continually slaughter nations without mercy?

NIV:

[14] You have made people like the fish in the sea,
like the sea creatures that have no ruler.
[15] The wicked foe pulls all of them up with hooks,
he catches them in his net,
he gathers them up in his dragnet;
and so he rejoices and is glad.
[16] Therefore he sacrifices to his net
and burns incense to his dragnet,
for by his net he lives in luxury
and enjoys the choicest food.

[17] Is he to keep on emptying his net,
 destroying nations without mercy?

NLT:

[14] Are we only fish to be caught and killed?
 Are we only sea creatures that have no leader?
[15] Must we be strung up on their hooks
 and caught in their nets while they rejoice and celebrate?
[16] Then they will worship their nets
 and burn incense in front of them.
"These nets are the gods who have made us rich!"
 they will claim.
[17] Will you let them get away with this forever?
 Will they succeed forever in their heartless conquests?

Paraphrase verses 14-17 in your own words:

What is his final complaint in verse 17?

4. In Habakkuk 2:1, what does he resolve to do?

5. Commentator James Montgomery Boice said, "A watch tower was often built in a grain field or vineyard to provide a place for a guard to keep an eye on the harvest...it could also be a tower in the city

where they could watch out for an enemy... A watch tower is something set apart or detached from the common press of life" (Boice, 1986, p.405).

How does this context about the watchtower help us understand what Habakkuk meant in verse 1?

Commentary

Habakkuk cried out for justice, and God gave him a stronger answer than he was expecting. When God shared His plans of judgement for Israel, Habakkuk was even more overwhelmed, confused, and distraught than before. So, he pressed further and continued his complaint to God. Habakkuk wrestles with this question: How could the circumstances of Judah's future fall to Babylon possibly align with God's *eternality* and His *purity*? Some of Habakkuk's straight-forward questions might make us uncomfortable—he is very bold. To cry in lament like this requires faith in a God who can handle grief and questions; Habakkuk knew and trusted that Yahweh was that God. With his faith to protect and guard him, the prophet pain-fully and earnestly searches the unfathomable wisdom of God. In doing so, he agonizes over some of the deepest questions that come with trusting a sovereign God while living in a broken world.

Verse 12

Habakkuk's first question was, "Are you not from everlasting, O Lord my God, my Holy One?" God had chosen to keep Israel as His own — and this, Habakkuk believed, was wrapped up in God's *everlasting* existence. When Habakkuk appeals to God's everlasting character, He is appealing to God's history of rescuing mercy to-ward Israel. Robertson suggests, "God was from eternity, and from eternity he had settled on a purpose." (Robertson, 1990, p. 157). In Habakkuk's mind, all the pictures God painted in His description of judgement pointed to possibilities of Judah being eradicated, and this deeply troubled him. How could God be everlasting and holy if he was planning to destroy His covenant people?

Habakkuk would have remembered God's record of the specific preservation of Judah in the past. He would have known the recent promise given in Micah 5:1, that a ruler would come out of

Bethlehem of Judah. He knew God had a purpose for Judah's future, so he wrestled and then concluded, "we shall not die." Habakkuk rests as he appeals to God's promise: Yahweh is *everlasting*, and the purposes of His heart will prevail. Yahweh is *Holy*, He will be true to His covenant — therefore, even with this dreadful news of judgement, God's people will not perish.

Even with the comfort of God's promise, Habakkuk acknowledged God had plans to severely judge Israel. And again, he leaned on God's faithfulness as he addressed Him as the "Rock," their safety and security. God established Babylon as a means of severe discipline for Israel, but Habakkuk submits and entrusts himself to Him as his Rock.

Verse 13

Habakkuk's trust in God's character leads him to be bold, and ask more questions. First, he appeals to God's purity and says, "You who are of purer eyes than to see evil and cannot look at wrong, why do you idly look at traitors and remain silent when the wicked swallows up the man more righteous than he?" Habakkuk is distraught because God's plan involves a wicked nation (Judah), being 'swallowed up' by an even more wicked nation (Babylon), and he questions how this aligns with God's purity. How could God deal with Judah's sin by using a method that appears to tolerate even more sin? Habakkuk utters deep profound questions of our faith that the Psalmists have echoed (Psalm 44:24), along with many others. His dilemma has been compared to a modern-day Christian crying out to God over the corruption of the church in America, to receive an answer from God that He has a plan to destroy the church by sending an anti-Christian, corrupt nation to conquer them (Boice, 1986, p. 400). At the heart of Habakkuk's wrestling is this: how could a Holy God's chosen people suffer at the hands of such depravity?

Verses 14-17

As he thinks about Babylon's reputation for violence, the gruesome nature of what might happen to his people also troubled Habakkuk. He acknowledges God's sovereign hand in the situation when he says, "*You* make mankind like the fish of the sea, like crawling things that have no ruler..." Habakkuk is pointing out that God has put them in a position where they will be forced to live as if they have no ruler. Judah will be made helpless, like the fish of the sea. Verses 15-17 tell us about the vicious and ruthless manner in which Babylon had dealt with their captives in the past. They gathered people mercilessly and repetitively as they pridefully rejoiced and lived in luxury. Not only that, but they see this practice as an act of worship to themselves (16). Habakkuk wearily asks in verse 17, "is he then to keep on emptying his net and killing nations forever?"

Chapter 2 verse 1

Habakkuk had thought through every possibility he could think of. He wrestled with God's word, and he knew he needed to leave the problem with God. He decides, "I will take my stand at my watch post and station myself on the tower." James Montgomery Boice gives context that helps us understand Habakkuk's imagery. A watchtower was often built in a grain field or a vineyard to provide a place for a guard to keep watch on a harvest. It could also be a tower from which a watchman would watch for an enemy during a time of war. Either way, a watchtower was set apart from the common activity and press of life (Boice, 1986, p. 405). Habakkuk had been in the trenches, used every reasoning method he knew, and asked God every question he could think of; he could not produce an answer on his own. It was time for him to detach himself from his questions and problems, pray, and wait for God's answer. He felt confident God would speak to him, and that God would offer him the wisdom he sought.

Interpretation: Seeing Jesus Christ in Habakkuk

1. Read **Genesis 49:8-10, Micah 5:2, and Matthew 2:3-6**. How is Habakkuk's hope that Judah "will not perish" wrapped up in the promise of the Jesus' coming?

8 "Judah, your brothers will praise you.
   You will grasp your enemies by the neck.
   All your relatives will bow before you.
9 Judah, my son, is a young lion
   that has finished eating its prey.
Like a lion he crouches and lies down;
   like a lioness—who dares to rouse him?
10 The scepter will not depart from Judah,
   nor the ruler's staff from his descendants,
until the coming of the one to whom it belongs,
   the one whom all nations will honor.
   and of Abraham:
   2 But you, O Bethlehem Ephrathah,
   who are too little to be among the clans of Judah,
from you shall come forth for me
   one who is to be ruler in Israel,
whose coming forth is from of old,
   from ancient days.

3 When Herod the king heard this, he was troubled, and all Jerusalem with him; 4 and assembling all the chief priests and scribes of the people, he inquired of them where the Christ was to be born. 5 They told him, "In Bethlehem of Judea, for so it is written by the prophet:

   6 "'And you, O Bethlehem, in the land of Judah,
   are by no means least among the rulers of Judah;

for from you shall come a ruler
   who will shepherd my people Israel.'"

2. In Habakkuk 1:12-2:1, the prophet prayed a prayer as he asked and waited for God's will amidst confusion and pain. Read the accounts of when Jesus made a similar prayer in **Matthew 26:36-56, Luke 22:42-46, Mark 14:32-42.** Fill out the following chart below as you compare Habakkuk's prayer with Jesus' prayer.

[36] Then Jesus went with them to a place called Gethsemane, and he said to his disciples, "Sit here, while I go over there and pray." [37] And taking with him Peter and the two sons of Zebedee, he began to be sorrowful and troubled. [38] Then he said to them, "My soul is very sorrowful, even to death; remain here, and watch[d]with me." [39] And going a little farther he fell on his face and prayed, saying, "My Father, if it be possible, let this cup pass from me; nevertheless, not as I will, but as you will." [40] And he came to the disciples and found them sleeping. And he said to Peter, "So, could you not watch with me one hour? [41] Watch and pray that you may not enter into temptation. The spirit indeed is willing, but the flesh is weak."[42] Again, for the second time, he went away and prayed, "My Father, if this cannot pass unless I drink it, your will be done." [43] And again he came and found them sleeping, for their eyes were heavy. [44] So, leaving them again, he went away and prayed for the third time, saying the same words again. [45] Then he came to the disciples and said to them, "Sleep and take your rest later on.[e] See, the hour is at hand, and the Son of Man is betrayed into the hands of sinners. [46] Rise, let us be going; see, my betrayer is at hand."

[47] While he was still speaking, Judas came, one of the twelve, and with him a great crowd with swords and clubs, from the chief priests and the elders of the people.[48] Now the betrayer had given them a sign, saying, "The one I will kiss is the man; seize him." [49] And he came up to Jesus at once and said, "Greetings, Rabbi!"

And he kissed him. [50] Jesus said to him, "Friend, do what you came to do."[f] Then they came up and laid hands on Jesus and seized him. [51] And behold, one of those who were with Jesus stretched out his hand and drew his sword and struck the servant[g] of the high priest and cut off his ear. [52] Then Jesus said to him, "Put your sword back into its place. For all who take the sword will perish by the sword.[53] Do you think that I cannot appeal to my Father, and he will at once send me more than twelve legions of angels? [54] But how then should the Scriptures be fulfilled, that it must be so?" [55] At that hour Jesus said to the crowds, "Have you come out as against a robber, with swords and clubs to capture me? Day after day I sat in the temple teaching, and you did not seize me. [56] But all this has taken place that the Scriptures of the prophets might be fulfilled." Then all the disciples left him and fled.

[41] And he withdrew from them about a stone's throw, and knelt down and prayed, [42] saying, "Father, if you are willing, remove this cup from me. Nevertheless, not my will, but yours, be done." [43] And there appeared to him an angel from heaven, strengthening him. [44] And being in agony he prayed more earnestly; and his sweat became like great drops of blood falling down to the ground. [45] And when he rose from prayer, he came to the disciples and found them sleeping for sorrow, [46] and he said to them, "Why are you sleeping? Rise and pray that you may not enter into temptation."

[32] And they went to a place called Gethsemane. And he said to his disciples, "Sit here while I pray." [33] And he took with him Peter and James and John, and began to be greatly distressed and troubled. [34] And he said to them, "My soul is very sorrowful, even to death. Remain here and watch."[a] [35] And going a little farther, he fell on the ground and prayed that, if it were possible, the hour might pass from him. [36] And he said, "Abba, Father, all things are possible for you. Remove this cup from me. Yet not what I will, but what you will." [37] And he came and found them sleeping, and he said to Peter,

"Simon, are you asleep? Could you not watch one hour? [38] Watch and pray that you may not enter into temptation. The spirit indeed is willing, but the flesh is weak." [39] And again he went away and prayed, saying the same words. [40] And again he came and found them sleeping, for their eyes were very heavy, and they did not know what to answer him. [41] And he came the third time and said to them, "Are you still sleeping and taking your rest? It is enough; the hour has come. The Son of Man is betrayed into the hands of sinners. [42] Rise, let us be going; see, my betrayer is at hand."

Habakkuk 1:12-2:1	Jesus in Matthew 26:36-56, Luke 22:42-46, Mark 14:32-42
The Address:	The Address:
The Request/Question:	The Request/Question:
The Conclusion:	The Conclusion:

3. How does Habakkuk point us to Jesus' greater lament and greater surrender?

Prayer & Journaling Prompt

Take some time to thank and praise Jesus that He...

Is the promised Savior from the line of Judah who secures the "yes and amen" to all of God's promises.

Cried out in holy lament regarding the hardship and suffering he was called to, and did so perfectly, so that when we cry out in our imperfect laments, we may be safe and held through our trust in His righteousness.

Trusted His Father's perfect will and promise, and was obedient to the point of death so that He might offer the hope of rescue to all who believe in Him.

Application & Reflection

1. In Habakkuk's experience, his understanding of God was not matching up with the circumstances he saw. Reflect on a time when you experienced confusion like this. How can you relate to Habakkuk's distress?

2. In perplexing circumstances, what attributes and/or promises of God have been a comfort and refuge for you?

How might the attributes of God fortify your faith in circumstances you are facing today?

3. Habakkuk's response to confusion was to appeal to God's promises, and *ask boldly*. How might God's character and promises, combined with your current circumstances, push you to ask boldly?

4. Reflect on the idea of Habakkuk "setting himself on a watchtower" in order to ask and wait for God's answer. How does this reflect a commitment to trust God?

5. Is there a circumstance in your life in which you need to take this step to wait for God's answer?

~ 4 ~

BY FAITH: THE WAY OF THE RIGHTEOUS

Observation & Interpretation

Habakkuk 2:1-5

Read Habakkuk 2:1-5 and consider the following questions.

2 I will take my stand at my watchpost
and station myself on the tower,
and look out to see what he will say to me,
and what I will answer concerning my complaint.
² And the Lord answered me:
"Write the vision;
make it plain on tablets,
so he may run who reads it.
³ For still the vision awaits its appointed time;
it hastens to the end—it will not lie.
If it seems slow, wait for it;
it will surely come; it will not delay.
⁴ "Behold, his soul is puffed up; it is not upright within him,
but the righteous shall live by his faith.

[5] "Moreover, wine is a traitor,
  an arrogant man who is never at rest.
His greed is as wide as Sheol;
  like death he has never enough.
He gathers for himself all nations
  and collects as his own all peoples."

1. Read verse 2. What are God's instructions to Habakkuk?

2. Some translations begin verse 3 with the word "For", which indicates a transition. What does verse 3 tell us about the reasons for God's instructions in verse 2?

3. In verses 4 and 5, God contrasts two kinds of people and 2 different ways of living. Record the motivations of the "righteous," and the "wicked" below.

    Righteous-

    Wicked-

4. God's instructions to live by faith in Habakkuk 2:4 would have reminded His people of His promise to Abraham. Read **Genesis**

15:1-6 and **Romans 4:16-22.** Describe what you think it meant for Abraham to live by faith.

15 After these things the word of the Lord came to Abram in a vision: "Fear not, Abram, I am your shield; your reward shall be very great." ² But Abram said, "O Lord God, what will you give me, for I continue childless, and the heir of my house is Eliezer of Damascus?" ³ And Abram said, "Behold, you have given me no offspring, and a member of my household will be my heir." ⁴ And behold, the word of the Lord came to him: "This man shall not be your heir; your very own son shall be your heir." ⁵ And he brought him outside and said, "Look toward heaven, and number the stars, if you are able to number them." Then he said to him, "So shall your offspring be." ⁶ And he believed the Lord, and he counted it to him as righteousness.

¹⁶ That is why it depends on faith, in order that the promise may rest on grace and be guaranteed to all his offspring—not only to the adherent of the law but also to the one who shares the faith of Abraham, who is the father of us all, ¹⁷ as it is written, "I have made you the father of many nations"—in the presence of the God in whom he believed, who gives life to the dead and calls into existence the things that do not exist. ¹⁸ In hope he believed against hope, that he should become the father of many nations, as he had been told, "So shall your offspring be." ¹⁹ He did not weaken in faith when he considered his own body, which was as good as dead (since he was about a hundred years old), or when he considered the barrenness of Sarah's womb. ²⁰ No unbelief made him waver concerning the promise of God, but he grew strong in his faith as he gave glory to God, ²¹ fully convinced that God was able to do what he had promised. ²² That is why his faith was "counted to him as righteousness."

5. Considering this context, what do you think it meant to Judah when they heard this command to live "by faith"?

Commentary

In the beginning of Chapter 2, Habakkuk surrendered and released his questions to God. Following the pattern of lament, His complaints had given way to bold questions (Vroegop), and he resolved to wait for God's answers. As we continue reading in verses 2-5, we see that God mercifully came to answer His prophet. God responded to Habakkuk's questions, and He shared how he planned to use Habakkuk to share truth with Israel. He begins with a warning and a preface as to just how significant this message was—this prophecy was to be shared with generations.

Verse 2

God said, "Write the vision; make it plain on tablets, so he may run who reads it." What God was about to share was a vision—it would come from outside Habakkuk. God emphasized that Habakkuk was to write it down and "make it plain." He was to relay the message in a way that was clear and helpful. Habakkuk had a responsibility to make sure God's people could easily read and understand this message. When we consider the history of God asking His prophets to "write on tablets," it reminds us of some of the most history-making messages in the Bible—the 10 commandments (Exodus 31:18), and Jesus' revelation of His return (Revelation 1:17-19) being among them. When God has a message for His covenant people to take hold of, he wants it to endure through generations, and he wants His words clear and plain for them to understand.

"So that he may run..." is a phrase associated with a prophet's assignment to spread the word. Prophets like Elisha and Zechariah were often told to take messages "and run". It meant to proclaim the message. (2 Kings 4:26 and Zechariah 2:4) (Robertson, 1990, p. 169) This vision of hope and redemption was to be written down in a way that could be easily spread.

Verse 3

Verse 3 begins with a transition word and tells us the reason it was so important that Habakkuk shared this message. "For still the vision awaits its appointed time; it hastens to the end—it will not lie. If it seems slow, wait for it; it will surely come; it will not delay." What God was about to reveal dealt with the future; it pertained to events that Habakkuk and Judah would have to wait for. It told of both the future of Judah as a nation, and the future of all humanity — and these events were certain. Waiting in confusing circumstances would make it difficult for God's people to endure with faith, so God graciously offered a clear message for them to take hold of. If Habakkuk wavered or experienced confusion over the slowness of God's timing, God encouraged him to wait—justice and redemption would surely come.

Verses 4 and 5

Habakkuk had cried out for justice; he agonized over both Judah's unrighteousness, and Babylon's wickedness. So, God responded and shared His view of justice, His view of righteousness, and how He will work out this righteousness over the earth.

Verse 4 contains a summary: "Behold, his soul is puffed up; it is not upright within him, but the righteous shall live by his faith." God compares two ways of living, and two different outcomes of these lifestyles. The first is the one whose "soul is puffed up..." he is not righteous before God. In the immediate context, God is referring to

Babylon. Verse 5 expands and tells us they live by their indulgence, selfishness, arrogance, and pride. And the other type of man is the righteous man, who "lives by his faith." He is motivated by faithfulness to God, and he is given life through his faith in God's salvation. This man's faith is not dependent on himself, but he entrusts himself to the mercy and righteousness of God. John Calvin helpfully explains that this faith, "strips us of all arrogance, and leads us naked and needy to God, that we may seek salvation from him alone, which would otherwise be far removed from us." (Calvin, 2005, p. 74). The theme of God's vision is that no human might or pride, even that of Babylon, will ever be able to save. Only faith in the God of justice and mercy will offer life and salvation. Only God's grace will provide righteousness. Come what may, this was to be the source of hope for the people of God.

This statement finds its roots in God's covenant to Abraham in Genesis 12—Israel was set apart, and made righteous, because of their faith in God. God reminded Habakkuk that this faith and grace would sustain them through exile, and ultimately it would be what would save them on the final day of God's judgement. On this side of the cross, we know we are justified, brought into God's covenant people, made righteous, and given salvation through our faith in Jesus Christ. Through our exile on this earth, and for the day of judgement, our hope is found in "living by faith" in the God of our salvation as He is revealed in Jesus Christ.

Interpretation: Seeing Jesus Christ in Habakkuk

1. The second portion of verse 4 is a foundational verse for Christians. James Montgomery Boice helpfully wrote that the three important Hebrew phrases in this verse are, "the righteous, or justified man", "shall live", and "by his faith" (Boice, 1986, pp.208-209).

Read **Romans 1:16-17, Hebrews 10:32-39,** and **Galatians 3:10-14** to consider places where this verse is quoted in the New Testament.

[16] For I am not ashamed of the gospel, for it is the power of God for salvation to everyone who believes, to the Jew first and also to the Greek. [17] For in it the righteousness of God is revealed from faith for faith, as it is written, "The righteous shall live by faith."

[32] But recall the former days when, after you were enlightened, you endured a hard struggle with sufferings, [33] sometimes being publicly exposed to reproach and affliction, and sometimes being partners with those so treated. [34] For you had compassion on those in prison, and you joyfully accepted the plundering of your property, since you knew that you yourselves had a better possession and an abiding one. [35] Therefore do not throw away your confidence, which has a great reward. [36] For you have need of endurance, so that when you have done the will of God you may receive what is promised. [37] For,
"Yet a little while,
and the coming one will come and will not delay;
[38] but my righteous one shall live by faith,
and if he shrinks back,
my soul has no pleasure in him."

[39] But we are not of those who shrink back and are destroyed, but of those who have faith and preserve their souls.

[10] For all who rely on works of the law are under a curse; for it is written, "Cursed be everyone who does not abide by all things written in the Book of the Law, and do them." [11] Now it is evident that no one is justified before God by the law, for "The righteous shall live by faith." [12] But the law is not of faith, rather "The one who does them shall live by them." [13] Christ redeemed us from the curse of the law by becoming a curse for us—for it is written, "Cursed is everyone who is hanged on a tree"— [14] so that in Christ Jesus the blessing of Abraham might come to the Gentiles, so that we might receive the promised Spirit through faith.

How do these New Testament interpretations shine light on the meaning of the following phrases...

The Righteous—

Shall live—

By his faith—

3. Considering this insight, write Habakkuk 2:4 in your own words.

4. Read **Ephesians 2:4-10** and consider the following questions.

[4] But God, being rich in mercy, because of the great love with which he loved us, [5] even when we were dead in our trespasses, made us alive together with Christ—by grace you have been saved— [6] and raised us up with him and seated us with him in the heavenly places in Christ Jesus, [7] so that in the coming ages he might show the immeasurable riches of his grace in kindness toward us in Christ Jesus. [8] For by grace you have been saved through faith. And this is not your own doing; it is the gift of God, [9] not a result of works, so that no one may boast. [10] For we are his workmanship, created in Christ Jesus for good works, which God prepared beforehand, that we should walk in them.

What does Paul say God has done to save us?

According to Ephesians 2:8-9, how do we receive the gift of salvation?

How does God's command for Habakkuk to live "by faith" point to Christ?

5. Read **Hebrews 12:1-3** and **Hebrews 4:14-16**. Underline the ways these verses describe how Jesus perfectly "lived by his faith" during adversity.

12 Therefore, since we are surrounded by so great a cloud of witnesses, let us also lay aside every weight, and sin which clings

so closely, and let us run with endurance the race that is set before us, ² looking to Jesus, the founder and perfecter of our faith, who for the joy that was set before him endured the cross, despising the shame, and is seated at the right hand of the throne of God. ³ Consider him who endured from sinners such hostility against himself, so that you may not grow weary or fainthearted.

¹⁴ Since then we have a great high priest who has passed through the heavens, Jesus, the Son of God, let us hold fast our confession. ¹⁵ For we do not have a high priest who is unable to sympathize with our weaknesses, but one who in every respect has been tempted as we are, yet without sin. ¹⁶ Let us then with confidence draw near to the throne of grace, that we may receive mercy and find grace to help in time of need.

How might His perfect faith on your behalf encourage you to rest when you are weary?

Prayer & Journal Prompt

Take some time to thank and praise Jesus that He is...

The perfect judge who displayed perfect justice through His death on the cross

The One in whom our faith rests—the one who became sin for us so that we might become the righteousness of God.

The one who lived by faith perfectly and endured the cross with faith in the joy set before Him, so that when we fail to live by faith, we may rest in Him.

Application & Reflection

1. God's command to His people, as they struggled with waiting and confusion, was for them to "live by his faith." Read the following promises that encourage us to live by faith on this side of the cross: **Romans 8:28-30, and 2 Corinthians 5:1-10.**

[28] And we know that for those who love God all things work together for good, for those who are called according to his purpose. [29] For those whom he foreknew he also predestined to be conformed to the image of his Son, in order that he might be the firstborn among many brothers. [30] And those whom he predestined he also called, and those whom he called he also justified, and those whom he justified he also glorified.

5 For we know that if the tent that is our earthly home is destroyed, we have a building from God, a house not made with hands, eternal in the heavens. [2] For in this tent we groan, longing to put on our heavenly dwelling, [3] if indeed by putting it on we may not be found naked. [4] For while we are still in this tent, we groan, being burdened—not that we would be unclothed, but that we would be further clothed, so that what is mortal may be swallowed up by life. [5] He who has prepared us for this very thing is God, who has given us the Spirit as a guarantee.

[6] So we are always of good courage. We know that while we are at home in the body we are away from the Lord, [7] for we walk by faith, not by sight. [8] Yes, we are of good courage, and we would rather be away from the body and at home with the Lord. [9] So whether we are at home or away, we make it our aim to please him. [10] For we must all appear before the judgment seat of Christ, so that each one may receive what is due for what he has done in the body, whether good or evil.

How might these provide encouragement in your calling to live by faith?

How might this call to live by faith influence your prayer life?

2. How is "living by faith" more challenging than living with prideful motivations?

Describe an area of your life where this tension has been difficult.

3. When circumstances seem confusing and painful, in what ways does living by faith in the Cross give you confidence?

How might this inform the way you view your trials today?

~ 5 ~

BY FAITH: WE TRUST GOD'S JUSTICE

Observation & Interpretation

Habakkuk 2:6-20

In Chapter 2, God answers Habakkuk's cry for justice by comparing the lives and rewards of the righteous versus the unrighteous. God explained that those who lived by faith in His mercy would be given life—but those who lived by their pride and selfishness were not righteous before God; they would experience His just judgment. In verses 6-20, God describes the judgment that unrighteous Babylon would receive. What we learn is that God administers an impartial, "eye for eye," kind of justice; Babylon would be treated according to the way they treated others. God's people would suffer severely under the rule of Babylon, so these "woes" would give them truth to claim during the hard days ahead. By faith, they could trust that God would be just. God promised to bring judgment on His peoples' enemies for His glory.

Read Habakkuk 2:6-20 and consider the following questions.

⁶ Shall not all these take up their taunt against him, with scoffing and riddles for him, and say,

"Woe to him who heaps up what is not his own—
for how long?—
and loads himself with pledges!"
⁷ Will not your debtors suddenly arise,
and those awake who will make you tremble?
Then you will be spoil for them.
⁸ Because you have plundered many nations,
all the remnant of the peoples shall plunder you,
for the blood of man and violence to the earth,
to cities and all who dwell in them.
⁹ "Woe to him who gets evil gain for his house,
to set his nest on high,
to be safe from the reach of harm!
¹⁰ You have devised shame for your house
by cutting off many peoples;
you have forfeited your life.
¹¹ For the stone will cry out from the wall,
and the beam from the woodwork respond.
¹² "Woe to him who builds a town with blood
and founds a city on iniquity!
¹³ Behold, is it not from the Lord of hosts
that peoples labor merely for fire,
and nations weary themselves for nothing?
¹⁴ For the earth will be filled
with the knowledge of the glory of the Lord
as the waters cover the sea.
¹⁵ "Woe to him who makes his neighbors drink—
you pour out your wrath and make them drunk,
in order to gaze at their nakedness!
¹⁶ You will have your fill of shame instead of glory.
Drink, yourself, and show your uncircumcision!
The cup in the Lord's right hand
will come around to you,
and utter shame will come upon your glory!

¹⁷ The violence done to Lebanon will overwhelm you,
   as will the destruction of the beasts that terrified them,
for the blood of man and violence to the earth,
   to cities and all who dwell in them.
    ¹⁸ "What profit is an idol
   when its maker has shaped it,
   a metal image, a teacher of lies?
For its maker trusts in his own creation
   when he makes speechless idols!
¹⁹ Woe to him who says to a wooden thing, Awake;
   to a silent stone, Arise!
Can this teach?
Behold, it is overlaid with gold and silver,
   and there is no breath at all in it.
²⁰ But the Lord is in his holy temple;
   let all the earth keep silence before him."

1. Verses 4-5 compared the lives of the wicked and the righteous, and verse 6 introduces a more detailed summary of wicked Babylon's future. Consider the following translations of verse 6a.

CSB: ⁶ Won't all of these take up a taunt against him,
with mockery and riddles about him?

NIV: ⁶ Will not all of them taunt him with ridicule and scorn, saying,

NLT: ⁶ "But soon their captives will taunt them.
   They will mock them, saying,

NKJV: ⁶ "Will not all these take up a proverb against him,
   And a taunting riddle against him, and say,

What does this tell you about the future of the relationship between Babylon and other nations?

2. Verses 6-20 detail the forthcoming judgment of Babylon. Record the "Woes" and the corresponding punishments below.

"Woe to him..."	Impending Result
Verses 6-8	
Verses 9-11	
Verses 12-14	
Verses 15-17	
Verses 18-20	

3. Consider Habakkuk 2:14 alongside **Isaiah 11:6-9** and **Psalm 72:18-19**. How does the future reality of God's glory filling the earth make Babylon's attempts worthless?

⁶ The wolf shall dwell with the lamb,
   and the leopard shall lie down with the young goat,
and the calf and the lion and the fattened calf together;
   and a little child shall lead them.
⁷ The cow and the bear shall graze;
   their young shall lie down together;
   and the lion shall eat straw like the ox.
⁸ The nursing child shall play over the hole of the cobra,
   and the weaned child shall put his hand on the adder's den.

⁹ They shall not hurt or destroy
   in all my holy mountain;
for the earth shall be full of the knowledge of the Lord
   as the waters cover the sea.

¹⁸ Blessed be the Lord, the God of Israel,
   who alone does wondrous things.
¹⁹ Blessed be his glorious name forever;
   may the whole earth be filled with his glory!
Amen and Amen!

4. How do you think these 5 oracles answer Habakkuk's complaint
in Habakkuk 1:12-17?

6. What stands out to you about the nature of God's justice?

7. What are God's instructions in verse 20?

Why do you think God's vision ends this way?

Commentary

Verse 6

The nature of Babylon's punishment is introduced, and verse 6 provides insight into the literary style of these judgment descriptions. Babylon will become a subject of taunting and riddles, and so the verses that follow are "woe" songs; they are written to be memorable, proverbial, and used as catchy riddles and taunts for Babylon's enemies. The Hebrew words in verses 7-20 reveal poetic elements like rhyming, alliteration, and proverbial language that are for "scoffing and riddles." Parallelism enhances the effectiveness of this poetic structure—these are meant to be memorable sayings (Robertson, 1990, p. 195). Israel was often warned that its destruction and downfall would become a taunt or a joke to other nations (Psalm 44:14). God revealed to Habakkuk that Babylon would also experience the justice of taunt and mockery.

Verses 6-8

Next comes the series of "woes." Verses 7-8 describe the judgement that will fall on Babylon for their plundering of nations. The Babylonians had plundered and stolen what was not theirs, so they would be plundered by other nations. They had ruthlessly taken from others, so God warned they would "be spoil for [those]" nations that they had taken from.

Verses 9-11

The leaders of Babylon were well known for being obsessively concerned about their dynasty—this is likely the meaning of the term "house" (Robertson, 1990, p. 192). Babylon was well known for using harmful and corrupt means to establish and preserve a name for themselves. Verse 9 says, "Woe to him who gets evil gain for his house, to set his nest on high, to be safe from the reach of harm!" Judgment was coming for those who only looked out for their own protection, their dynasty, and their reputation. Their ambition was their legacy and they looked for ways to honor their own names—but in their "cutting off" of others, they only brought shame upon themselves. Babylon may have thought their selfishness was discrete, but verse 11 says that witnesses would speak out against them. The king's dynasty would fall to pieces, no matter the strength of their own efforts.

Verses 12-14

Building a city based on sinful and violent practices, selfishness, and the glory of man is totally in vain. Psalm 127:1 tells us that unless a house is built by the Lord, those who build it build it in vain. No matter the amount of effort put into building a city, it will be pointless if it is not for the Lord's glory. Babylon would go to great lengths and efforts to build cities for their own name—and it would end in deep shame and destruction. Verse 13 says, "Behold, is it not from the LORD of hosts that peoples labor merely for fire, and nations weary themselves for nothing?" God warns that Babylon, along with every culture who prides themselves in building a city for the sake of self, would experience fire and judgement. Hidden and selfish motives will be brought to light, exposed, and judged in the end.

Why is it so futile to build something for the glory of ourselves? Because God's purpose is that the whole earth would be filled with *His* glory. Verse 14 tells us where we are all headed, "The earth will be filled with the knowledge of the glory of the Lord like the waters cover the sea." The events that Habakkuk would witness in his day would be a profound demonstration of God revealing His glory. Babylon's destruction and righteous judgement provided great relief to a troubled world (Robertson, 1990, p. 199) (Daniel 5). *Yet, Habakkuk's words here anticipate something greater that's still to come.*

Since the beginning, God has had a plan to bless the world with His glory and grace. He has been revealing himself and pursuing His people since Genesis; revealing more and more of His glory through His word and His prophets. Through Jesus' life, death, and resurrection, we see more of His glory. And through Jesus' payment of man's sin on the cross, God dealt with the sin of the world, and is continuing to transform His people, by His spirit, from one degree of glory to another (2 Corinthians 3:18). He is making all things new to prepare a place where the problem of the wicked will be resolved forever, and the glory of the Lord, through Christ, will cover the earth as the waters cover the sea.

Verses 15-17

These verses paint a terrible and gruesome picture of the manipulative motives of the wicked. Verse 15 says, "Woe to him who makes his neighbors drink-- you pour out your wrath and make them drunk, in order to gaze at their nakedness!" In their depravity, the Babylonians use methods like alcohol in order to abuse, humiliate, and shame their victims. Understandably, verse 16 tells us Babylon would experience "utter shame" for their actions.

Verse 17 addresses "the violence done against Lebanon," and it helps us to know some context. Other parts of scripture tell us that the forests of Lebanon were well known for their proverbial beauty, and Babylon ruthlessly cut down these trees for their massive building projects. (ESV Study Bible). Psalm 104:16 references God planting the trees of Lebanon himself; they were majestic, and representative of God's glory and beauty in creation. Babylon would be judged for both their treatment of humanity, and their ruthless destruction of God's creation.

Verses 18-20

The last judgement deals with idolatry. God thoroughly articulates the futility and deception of this practice. There is no logic or profit in worshiping a man-made, lifeless creation—idolatry is "a teacher of lies" and blinding to those who practice it. Verses 18-19 describe the danger and stupidity of someone expecting a silent stone to teach them. This is exactly what Babylon did, and it's what everyone who puts their hope and trust in a man-made creation is guilty of doing. No matter how beautiful and valuable the idol is made to look, it is lifeless.

Verse 20 concludes by declaring that, in contrast to these lifeless idols, the God of Judah is alive and present in His temple. He is not silent, but He speaks and is ready to instruct His people. And in response, the whole earth is silenced in reverential awe before Him.

Interpretation: Seeing Jesus in Habakkuk

1. List some ways that God's warning in Habakkuk 2:12-14 is similar to the Apostle Paul's warning in **1 Corinthians 3:11-15**, and Jesus' warning in **Matthew 7:24-27**.

[11] For no one can lay a foundation other than that which is laid, which is Jesus Christ. [12] Now if anyone builds on the foundation with gold, silver, precious stones, wood, hay, straw— [13] each one's work will become manifest, for the Day will disclose it, because it will be revealed by fire, and the fire will test what sort of work each one has done. [14] If the work that anyone has built on the foundation survives, he will receive a reward. [15] If anyone's work is burned up, he will suffer loss, though he himself will be saved, but only as through fire.

24 "Everyone then who hears these words of mine and does them will be like a wise man who built his house on the rock. 25 And the rain fell, and the floods came, and the winds blew and beat on that house, but it did not fall, because it had been founded on the rock. 26 And everyone who hears these words of mine and does not do them will be like a foolish man who built his house on the sand.27 And the rain fell, and the floods came, and the winds blew and beat against that house, and it fell, and great was the fall of it."

2. Read **Matthew 23:13-15, 27-28.** What do you observe about Jesus' hatred for unjust use of power?

13 "But woe to you, scribes and Pharisees, hypocrites! For you shut the kingdom of heaven in people's faces. For you neither enter yourselves nor allow those who would enter to go in. 15 Woe to you, scribes and Pharisees, hypocrites! For you travel across sea and land to make a single proselyte, and when he becomes a proselyte, you make him twice as much a child of hell as yourselves.

27 "Woe to you, scribes and Pharisees, hypocrites! For you are like whitewashed tombs, which outwardly appear beautiful, but within are full of dead people's bones and all uncleanness. 28 So you also outwardly appear righteous to others, but within you are full of hypocrisy and lawlessness.

How does Jesus' desire for justice reflect the passion demonstrated by the woe songs of Habakkuk 2:6-20?

3. Read more about this future reality of God's glory filling the earth (Habakkuk 2:14) in **Revelation 21:22-22:5**. Record your observations about this promise.

[22] And I saw no temple in the city, for its temple is the Lord God the Almighty and the Lamb. [23] And the city has no need of sun or moon to shine on it, for the glory of God gives it light, and its lamp is the Lamb. [24] By its light will the nations walk, and the kings of the earth will bring their glory into it, [25] and its gates will never be shut by day—and there will be no night there. [26] They will bring into it the glory and the honor of the nations. [27] But nothing unclean will ever enter it, nor anyone who does what is detestable or false, but only those who are written in the Lamb's book of life.

22 Then the angel showed me the river of the water of life, bright as crystal, flowing from the throne of God and of the Lamb [2] through the middle of the street of the city; also, on either side of the river, the tree of life with its twelve kinds of fruit, yielding its fruit each month. The leaves of the tree were for the healing of the nations. [3] No longer will there be anything accursed, but the throne of God and of the Lamb will be in it, and his servants will worship him. [4] They will see his face, and his name will be on their foreheads. [5] And night will be no more. They will need no light of lamp or sun, for the Lord God will be their light, and they will reign forever and ever.

How does Habakkuk 2:12-14 point to both God's justice and our hope?

How does the promised future in Revelation offer consolation as we wrestle with injustice?

Prayer & Journal Prompt

Take some time to thank and praise Jesus that He is...

The One who makes God's glorious justice, mercy, love, and holiness known through His life of service and His work on the cross.

The One who ushered in a Kingdom filled with the knowledge of the Glory of God through His sacrifice for sin.

The One who has secured a New Heaven and a New Earth, where justice is final and the Glory of God will be our light "as the waters cover the sea..."

Application & Reflection

1. God pronounced woe on unjust and abusive use of power. Where do you see this kind of injustice in our world today?

2. God is passionate about justice. Through Christ, He promises to right every wrong for Habakkuk's people and for us. How does God's passion for justice comfort you?

How does God's passion for justice convict you?

3. Read **Psalm 73** and consider how the psalmist's wrestling over the "prosperity of the wicked" is similar to Habakkuk's questioning.

> 73 Truly God is good to Israel,
>   to those who are pure in heart.
> ² But as for me, my feet had almost stumbled,
>   my steps had nearly slipped.
> ³ For I was envious of the arrogant
>   when I saw the prosperity of the wicked.
>   ⁴ For they have no pangs until death;
>   their bodies are fat and sleek.
> ⁵ They are not in trouble as others are;
>   they are not stricken like the rest of mankind.
> ⁶ Therefore pride is their necklace;
>   violence covers them as a garment.

⁷ Their eyes swell out through fatness;
   their hearts overflow with follies.
⁸ They scoff and speak with malice;
   loftily they threaten oppression.
⁹ They set their mouths against the heavens,
   and their tongue struts through the earth.
¹⁰ Therefore his people turn back to them,
   and find no fault in them.
¹¹ And they say, "How can God know?
   Is there knowledge in the Most High?"
¹² Behold, these are the wicked;
   always at ease, they increase in riches.
¹³ All in vain have I kept my heart clean
   and washed my hands in innocence.
¹⁴ For all the day long I have been stricken
   and rebuked every morning.
¹⁵ If I had said, "I will speak thus,"
   I would have betrayed the generation of your children.
      ¹⁶ But when I thought how to understand this,
   it seemed to me a wearisome task,
¹⁷ until I went into the sanctuary of God;
   then I discerned their end.
      ¹⁸ Truly you set them in slippery places;
   you make them fall to ruin.
¹⁹ How they are destroyed in a moment,
   swept away utterly by terrors!
²⁰ Like a dream when one awakes,
   O Lord, when you rouse yourself, you despise them as phantoms.
²¹ When my soul was embittered,
   when I was pricked in heart,
²² I was brutish and ignorant;
   I was like a beast toward you.
      ²³ Nevertheless, I am continually with you;
   you hold my right hand.

²⁴ You guide me with your counsel,
and afterward you will receive me to glory.
²⁵ Whom have I in heaven but you?
And there is nothing on earth that I desire besides you.
²⁶ My flesh and my heart may fail,
but God is the strength of my heart and my portion forever.
²⁷ For behold, those who are far from you shall perish;
you put an end to everyone who is unfaithful to you.
²⁸ But for me it is good to be near God;
I have made the Lord God my refuge,
that I may tell of all your works.

How is his wrestling resolved in Psalm 73:23-28?

How do you think Asaph's source of peace relates to God's instructions in Habakkuk 2:20?

3. How does the reality of God's glory "filling the earth as the waters cover the sea" inform the way you view your ambitions?

How might this reality inform your prayer for your life?

How might this inform your prayer for others?

~ 6 ~

BY FAITH: WE TRUST GOD'S SALVATION

Observation & Interpretation

Habakkuk 3:1-15

Read Habakkuk 3:1-15 and consider the following questions.

3 A prayer of Habakkuk the prophet, according to Shigionoth.
² O Lord, I have heard the report of you,
and your work, O Lord, do I fear.
In the midst of the years revive it;
in the midst of the years make it known;
in wrath remember mercy.
³ God came from Teman,
and the Holy One from Mount Paran. Selah
His splendor covered the heavens,
and the earth was full of his praise.
⁴ His brightness was like the light;
rays flashed from his hand;
and there he veiled his power.
⁵ Before him went pestilence,
and plague followed at his heels.
⁶ He stood and measured the earth;

he looked and shook the nations;
then the eternal mountains were scattered;
   the everlasting hills sank low.
   His were the everlasting ways.
[7] I saw the tents of Cushan in affliction;
   the curtains of the land of Midian did tremble.
[8] Was your wrath against the rivers, O Lord?
   Was your anger against the rivers,
   or your indignation against the sea,
when you rode on your horses,
   on your chariot of salvation?
[9] You stripped the sheath from your bow,
   calling for many arrows. Selah
   You split the earth with rivers.
[10] The mountains saw you and writhed;
   the raging waters swept on;
the deep gave forth its voice;
   it lifted its hands on high.
[11] The sun and moon stood still in their place
   at the light of your arrows as they sped,
   at the flash of your glittering spear.
[12] You marched through the earth in fury;
   you threshed the nations in anger.
[13] You went out for the salvation of your people,
   for the salvation of your anointed.
You crushed the head of the house of the wicked,
   laying him bare from thigh to neck. Selah
[14] You pierced with his own arrows the heads of his warriors,
   who came like a whirlwind to scatter me,
   rejoicing as if to devour the poor in secret.
[15] You trampled the sea with your horses,
   the surging of mighty waters.

1. Chapter 3 contains Habakkuk's response of worship. What does verse 1 tell us about this Chapter?

2. Read the following translations of Habakkuk 3:1-2.

NIV:

> 3 A prayer of Habakkuk the prophet. On *shigionoth*.
>
> ^{2} Lord, I have heard of your fame;
> I stand in awe of your deeds, Lord.
> Repeat them in our day,
>   in our time make them known;
>   in wrath remember mercy.

CSB:

> 3 A prayer of the prophet Habakkuk. According to *Shigionoth*.
>
> ^{2} Lord, I have heard the report about you;
> Lord, I stand in awe of your deeds.
> Revive your work in these years;
> make it known in these years.
> In your wrath remember mercy!

NLT:

> 3 This prayer was sung by the prophet Habakkuk:
>
> ^{2} I have heard all about you, Lord.
> I am filled with awe by your amazing works.
> In this time of our deep need,
>   help us again as you did in years gone by.
> And in your anger,
>   remember your mercy.

NKJV:

3 A prayer of Habakkuk the prophet, on Shigionoth.

² O Lord, I have heard Your speech *and* was afraid;

O Lord, revive Your work in the midst of the years!

In the midst of the years make *it* known;

In wrath remember mercy.

Paraphrase Habakkuk's plea in your own words:

3. Habakkuk wrote a song for Israel that created a collage of pictures of God's redemption. He does this by recalling God's work on behalf of His people, and looking toward God's future deliverance of His people. It's difficult to understand what specific events Habakkuk describes, but we can gain some insight by reading other parts of scripture that reference events like the ones in Habakkuk's prayer. Use the following passages to fill out the chart. This will help you gain an understanding of God's salvation patterns described in Habakkuk and throughout the Bible.

Psalm 105:26-38

²⁶ He sent Moses his servant,

and Aaron, whom he had chosen.

²⁷ They performed his signs among them,

his wonders in the land of Ham.

²⁸ He sent darkness and made the land dark—

for had they not rebelled against his words?

²⁹ He turned their waters into blood,

causing their fish to die.

³⁰ Their land teemed with frogs,

which went up into the bedrooms of their rulers.

[31] He spoke, and there came swarms of flies,
   and gnats throughout their country.
[32] He turned their rain into hail,
   with lightning throughout their land;
[33] he struck down their vines and fig trees
   and shattered the trees of their country.
[34] He spoke, and the locusts came,
   grasshoppers without number;
[35] they ate up every green thing in their land,
   ate up the produce of their soil.
[36] Then he struck down all the firstborn in their land,
   the firstfruits of all their manhood.
[37] He brought out Israel, laden with silver and gold,
   and from among their tribes no one faltered.
[38] Egypt was glad when they left,
   because dread of Israel had fallen on them.
   [39] He spread out a cloud as a covering,
   and a fire to give light at night.

Deuteronomy 33:2
[2] He said:
"The Lord came from Sinai
and dawned over them from Seir;
he shone forth from Mount Paran.
He came with myriads of holy ones
   from the south, from his mountain slopes.

Revelation 1:7
[7] "Look, he is coming with the clouds,"
and "every eye will see him,
even those who pierced him";
   and all peoples on earth "will mourn because of him."
So shall it be! Amen.

Exodus 14:21-31

²¹ Then Moses stretched out his hand over the sea, and all that night the Lorddrove the sea back with a strong east wind and turned it into dry land. The waters were divided, ²² and the Israelites went through the sea on dry ground, with a wallof water on their right and on their left.

²³ The Egyptians pursued them, and all Pharaoh's horses and chariots and horsemen followed them into the sea. ²⁴ During the last watch of the night the Lord looked down from the pillar of fire and cloud at the Egyptian army and threw it into confusion. ²⁵ He jammed the wheels of their chariots so that they had difficulty driving. And the Egyptians said, "Let's get away from the Israelites! The Lord is fighting for them against Egypt."

²⁶ Then the Lord said to Moses, "Stretch out your hand over the sea so that the waters may flow back over the Egyptians and their chariots and horsemen."²⁷ Moses stretched out his hand over the sea, and at daybreak the sea went back to its place. The Egyptians were fleeing toward it, and the Lord swept them into the sea. ²⁸ The water flowed back and covered the chariots and horsemen—the entire army of Pharaoh that had followed the Israelites into the sea. Not one of them survived.

²⁹ But the Israelites went through the sea on dry ground, with a wall of water on their right and on their left. ³⁰ That day the Lord saved Israel from the hands of the Egyptians, and Israel saw the Egyptians lying dead on the shore. ³¹ And when the Israelites saw the mighty hand of the Lord displayed against the Egyptians, the people feared the Lord and put their trust in him and in Moses his servant.

Psalm 106:7-12

When our ancestors were in Egypt,
    they gave no thought to your miracles;

they did not remember your many kindnesses,
   and they rebelled by the sea, the Red Sea.
⁸ Yet he saved them for his name's sake,
   to make his mighty power known.
⁹ He rebuked the Red Sea, and it dried up;
   he led them through the depths as through a desert.
¹⁰ He saved them from the hand of the foe;
   from the hand of the enemy he redeemed them.
¹¹ The waters covered their adversaries;
   not one of them survived.
¹² Then they believed his promises
   and sang his praise.

Joshua 10:6-14

⁶ The Gibeonites then sent word to Joshua in the camp at Gilgal: "Do not abandon your servants. Come up to us quickly and save us! Help us, because all the Amorite kings from the hill country have joined forces against us."

⁷ So Joshua marched up from Gilgal with his entire army, including all the best fighting men. ⁸ The Lord said to Joshua, "Do not be afraid of them; I have given them into your hand. Not one of them will be able to withstand you."

⁹ After an all-night march from Gilgal, Joshua took them by surprise. ¹⁰ The Lord threw them into confusion before Israel, so Joshua and the Israelites defeated them completely at Gibeon. Israel pursued them along the road going up to Beth Horon and cut them down all the way to Azekah and Makkedah. ¹¹ As they fled before Israel on the road down from Beth Horon to Azekah, the Lord hurled large hailstones down on them, and more of them died from the hail than were killed by the swords of the Israelites.

¹² On the day the Lord gave the Amorites over to Israel, Joshua said to the Lord in the presence of Israel:

   "Sun, stand still over Gibeon,
   and you, moon, over the Valley of Aijalon."

[13] So the sun stood still,
  and the moon stopped,
  till the nation avenged itself on its enemies,
    as it is written in the Book of Jashar.

The sun stopped in the middle of the sky and delayed going down about a full day. [14] There has never been a day like it before or since, a day when the Lord listened to a human being. Surely the Lord was fighting for Israel!

2 Samuel 7:11-16

[10] And I will provide a place for my people Israel and will plant them so that they can have a home of their own and no longer be disturbed. Wicked people will not oppress them anymore, as they did at the beginning [11] and have done ever since the time I appointed leaders over my people Israel. I will also give you rest from all your enemies.

"'The Lord declares to you that the Lord himself will establish a house for you:[12] When your days are over and you rest with your ancestors, I will raise up your offspring to succeed you, your own flesh and blood, and I will establish his kingdom. [13] He is the one who will build a house for my Name, and I will establish the throne of his kingdom forever. [14] I will be his father, and he will be my son. When he does wrong, I will punish him with a rod wielded by men, with floggings inflicted by human hands. [15] But my love will never be taken away from him, as I took it away from Saul, whom I removed from before you. [16] Your house and your kingdom will endure forever before me; your throne will be established forever.'"

Psalm 89:3-4

[3] You said, "I have made a covenant with my chosen one,
    I have sworn to David my servant,
  [4] 'I will establish your line forever
    and make your throne firm through all generations.'"

Psalm 2

2 Why do the nations rage
and the peoples plot in vain?

[2] The kings of the earth set themselves,
and the rulers take counsel together,
against the Lord and against his Anointed, saying,

[3] "Let us burst their bonds apart
and cast away their cords from us."

[4] He who sits in the heavens laughs;
the Lord holds them in derision.

[5] Then he will speak to them in his wrath,
and terrify them in his fury, saying,

[6] "As for me, I have set my King
on Zion, my holy hill."

[7] I will tell of the decree:
The Lord said to me, "You are my Son;
today I have begotten you.

[8] Ask of me, and I will make the nations your heritage,
and the ends of the earth your possession.

[9] You shall break them with a rod of iron
and dash them in pieces like a potter's vessel."

[10] Now therefore, O kings, be wise;
be warned, O rulers of the earth.

[11] Serve the Lord with fear,
and rejoice with trembling.

[12] Kiss the Son,
lest he be angry, and you perish in the way,
for his wrath is quickly kindled.
Blessed are all who take refuge in him.

Scripture References	What events are described?	What characteristics of God are revealed by these events?
Habakkuk 3:3-7, Psalm 105:26-38 Deuteronomy 33:2 Revelation 1:7		
Habakkuk 3: 8-11, Exodus 14:21-31, Psalm 106:7-12, Joshua 10:6-14		
Habakkuk 3:12-15, 2 Samuel 7:11-16, Psalm 89:3-4, Psalm 2		

3. How do you think recalling these events in Israel's history and looking to God's promises for the future helped give Habakkuk relief and strengthen his faith?

Commentary

As the final chapter opens, we see that God graciously gives His people a tool to help them wait with hope in adversity. The first verse opens with the term "shigionoth," which is a word we see in the Psalms; it's most likely a genre of song or instrument (ESV Study Bible). In verses 3, 9, and 13 we read the word "Selah," which is believed to be a term that prompted pause and reflection during a service of worship. And the very last part of the last verse of Habakkuk instructs that 3:1-19 are to be given, "To the choirmaster: with stringed instruments." As Israel waited for the events in Habakkuk's prophecy to unfold, they were given a song to remind them of God's redemption; God gave them words to rehearse so that they might cling to His instructions to "live by faith" in His Salvation.

We know that Habakkuk 3 was intended to stir the Israelites hearts to praise, and this suggests that we should receive it that way too. This chapter is a vision or message that Habakkuk receives from God, formatted into a prayer. Habakkuk wrote a liturgy that incited images of God's deliverance, and led His people to trust and worship God. Many scholars have debated what specific events Habakkuk refers to. While it is not widely agreed upon whether Habakkuk is referring to the deliverance in the Old Testament or a vision of God's final deliverance in the future—biblical patterns, specifically of songs like the ones written by Moses and Deborah, (Deuteronomy 31 and Judges 6), help us understand that imagery in biblical songs probably refer to the past, present, *and* future of God's people. We do not know all the specific acts described in chapter 3, but it's clear that the illustrations and events Habakkuk shared make a picture collage of God as Savior.

Habakkuk had poured out his heart in lament, and God's answer revealed He was even more Holy, even more Just, and even more of a trustworthy and powerful Savior than anyone could have ever expected. Habakkuk's honest prayer of pain had led him to trust and worship. In this final Chapter, we see more clearly how Habakkuk, and all of God's people might "live by faith" amid painful and confusing circumstances. God has always been and always will be a God who sees, comes, and uses His saving power to intervene on behalf of His people.

Verses 1-2

Habakkuk begins by telling God about how he responded when he heard His words. He heard God's answer and experienced belief and deep and reverent fear. He accepted God's righteous plans, and asked God to, "In the midst of the years revive it; in the midst of the years make it known..." The prophet asked for God to remember, make known to all, and do His righteous work as they waited for His deliverance. Then he pleaded, "in wrath, remember mercy..." Habakkuk had learned of the dark, fear-filled exile God's people were about to face—and he knew the only way that he and others would "live by faith" during these years was by God's faithfulness. Nothing could sustain them except for God's undeserved mercy.

Verses 3-7

Habakkuk's praise details Israel's Hope. The first phrase says, "God came..." and God's people will recall that every instance of His saving mercy has been initiated by the God who *comes* to us. It is this same gracious coming that Habakkuk recalled, prophesied, and illustrated in Habakkuk 3.

Habakkuk reports that "he came from Teman, and the Holy One from Mount Paran..." These connections point us to when God led his people to inherit the promised land. Teman is geographically southern and associated with Edom, and Paran designates the Sinai wilderness and Egypt" (Fentress, 2018, p. 206). God showed His deliverance and kept His promise to bless them when He brought them out of Egypt. Habakkuk clings to this solid image of God's rescue as he attempts to describe God's promise of rescue in the future. After God brought His people out of Egypt, He appeared to Moses in glorious splendor and light, and He "veiled his power" to protect Israel from His full glory (Exodus 19, 20, and 34). This is the same imagery Habakkuk gives in verses 3b-4, "His splendor covered the heavens, and the earth was full of his praise. His brightness was like the light; rays flashed from his hand; and there he veiled his power."

God's coming has always marked by the reality that He is light. Amidst the darkness of Judah's exile under Babylon, He would come and shine gloriously and brightly. Isaiah prophesied in Isaiah 9 of Christ's coming, "the people in darkness [would] see a great light," and Jesus himself confirmed he was the light of the world (John 8:12). Jesus also promised a day when He will return in splendor and "as lightning that comes from the east is visible even in the west, so will be the coming of the Son of Man" (Matthew 24:27). When God rescues, He comes as the light.

Verses 5 and 6 remind us again of the Exodus from Egypt, and also of God's last rescue of His people in Revelation 11. God uses weapons of "plagues...pestilence" and earthquakes to "shake the nations" and reveal that He is the One true God, and His are the "everlasting ways."

Verses 8-11

Imagery in verses 8-11 comforts Israel with memories of God's power over nature on their behalf. When God demonstrated power over the Red Sea to deliver Israel, He was not merely showing "wrath against the rivers," but He was moving all creation for the rescue and redemption of His people. Rivers were often boundary ways into new lands, and God bringing His people through rivers and seas reminds us of Him keeping His promises to bring His people to the land He prepared for them (Joshua 1:11) (Robertson, 1990, p. 231). And after He brought Joshua into the land, God displayed His power over the cosmos when "The sun and moon stood still in their place", and God fought for Joshua to win the battle (Joshua 10). This powerful memory alongside Jesus' power over the sun and moon at His victorious coming in Revelation 8 leads us to worship — come what may, God is a rescuer who moves both cosmic and earthly powers for the salvation of His people.

Verses 12-15

Habakkuk continues to depict God as a valiant warrior who "in wrath, strode through the earth... crushes the wicked... and pierces with arrows." God's purpose is, "for the salvation of your people, for the salvation of [His] anointed." God's purpose in moving as a mighty warrior is clear—He is a God who keeps His covenant with His chosen people, "His anointed." Habakkuk received God's message with a deep worship and trust. God's news of His judgement of Israel had been severe, but when Habakkuk thought about the memories and future promises of God's glorious salvation, he was empowered to "live by faith."

Interpretation: Seeing Jesus Christ in Habakkuk

In the New Covenant, we know that the songs of salvation of the Old Testament are a shadow of the work of Christ. Use the following verses in the NT to help you fill out the chart below.

Colossians 2:13-15

[13] When you were dead in your sins and in the uncircumcision of your flesh, God made you alive with Christ. He forgave us all our sins, [14] having canceled the charge of our legal indebtedness, which stood against us and condemned us; he has taken it away, nailing it to the cross. [15] And having disarmed the powers and authorities, he made a public spectacle of them, triumphing over them by the cross.

1 Peter 1:18-21

[18] knowing that you were ransomed from the futile ways inherited from your forefathers, not with perishable things such as silver or gold, [19] but with the precious blood of Christ, like that of a lamb without blemish or spot. [20] He was foreknown before the foundation of the world but was made manifest in the last times for the sake of you [21] who through him are believers in God, who raised him from the dead and gave him glory, so that your faith and hope are in God.

Ephesians 1:7-14

[7] In him we have redemption through his blood, the forgiveness of our trespasses, according to the riches of his grace, [8] which he lavished upon us, in all wisdom and insight [9] making known to us the mystery of his will, according to his purpose, which he set forth in Christ [10] as a plan for the fullness of time, to unite all things in him, things in heaven and things on earth.

[11] In him we have obtained an inheritance, having been predestined according to the purpose of him who works all things

according to the counsel of his will, [12] so that we who were the first to hope in Christ might be to the praise of his glory. [13] In him you also, when you heard the word of truth, the gospel of your salvation, and believed in him, were sealed with the promised Holy Spirit, [14] who is the guarantee of our inheritance until we acquire possession of it, to the praise of his glory.

Ephesians 2:1-10

2 And you were dead in the trespasses and sins [2] in which you once walked, following the course of this world, following the prince of the power of the air, the spirit that is now at work in the sons of disobedience— [3] among whom we all once lived in the passions of our flesh, carrying out the desires of the body and the mind, and were by nature children of wrath, like the rest of mankind. [4] But God, being rich in mercy, because of the great love with which he loved us, [5] even when we were dead in our trespasses, made us alive together with Christ—by grace you have been saved— [6] and raised us up with him and seated us with him in the heavenly places in Christ Jesus, [7] so that in the coming ages he might show the immeasurable riches of his grace in kindness toward us in Christ Jesus. [8] For by grace you have been saved through faith. And this is not your own doing; it is the gift of God, [9] not a result of works, so that no one may boast. [10] For we are his workmanship, created in Christ Jesus for good works, which God prepared beforehand, that we should walk in them.

Revelation 5

5 Then I saw in the right hand of him who sat on the throne a scroll with writing on both sides and sealed with seven seals. [2] And I saw a mighty angel proclaiming in a loud voice, "Who is worthy to break the seals and open the scroll?" [3] But no one in heaven or on earth or under the earth could open the scroll or even look inside it. [4] I wept and wept because no one was found who was worthy to

open the scroll or look inside. ⁵ Then one of the elders said to me, "Do not weep! See, the Lion of the tribe of Judah, the Root of David, has triumphed. He is able to open the scroll and its seven seals."

⁶ Then I saw a Lamb, looking as if it had been slain, standing at the center of the throne, encircled by the four living creatures and the elders. The Lamb had seven horns and seven eyes, which are the seven spirits of God sent out into all the earth. ⁷ He went and took the scroll from the right hand of him who sat on the throne. ⁸ And when he had taken it, the four living creatures and the twenty-four elders fell down before the Lamb. Each one had a harp and they were holding golden bowls full of incense, which are the prayers of God's people. ⁹ And they sang a new song, saying:

"You are worthy to take the scroll
and to open its seals,
because you were slain,
and with your blood you purchased for God
persons from every tribe and language and people and nation.
¹⁰ You have made them to be a kingdom and priests to serve our God,
and they will reign on the earth."

¹¹ Then I looked and heard the voice of many angels, numbering thousands upon thousands, and ten thousand times ten thousand. They encircled the throne and the living creatures and the elders. ¹² In a loud voice they were saying:

"Worthy is the Lamb, who was slain,
to receive power and wealth and wisdom and strength
and honor and glory and praise!"

¹³ Then I heard every creature in heaven and on earth and under the earth and on the sea, and all that is in them, saying:

"To him who sits on the throne and to the Lamb
be praise and honor and glory and power,
for ever and ever!"

¹⁴ The four living creatures said, "Amen," and the elders fell down and worshiped.

Fill out the following chart and consider how Jesus reveals the full picture of the "God of our salvation." (Habakkuk 3:18)

Scripture References	What did Jesus save us **from**, what does He save us **to**, and/or what does He promise to rescue us from in the future?	What characteristics of Jesus are revealed by this salvation?
Colossians 2:13-15		
1 Peter 1:18-21		
Ephesians 1:7-14		
Ephesians 2:1-10		
Revelation 5		

Prayer & Journal Prompt

Take some time to thank and praise Jesus that He is...

The Lamb who was slain for our sin, and the Lion who conquers sin and death, achieving for us Salvation.

The One who frees us from the slavery of sin, accomplishes our salvation, and secures for us an inheritance in heaven with no tears, suffering, or pain.

Application & Reflection

1. What are your thoughts about the fact that in order to help His people "live by faith," God gave Judah a song to sing?

How does this inform the way we receive Habakkuk 3?

How has God moved in your heart through songs?

4. How are you given comfort and encouragement by God as the "warrior of salvation"?

How might this example of lament and worship influence your own prayer life?

5. What would it mean for you to live by faith in the God of Salvation this week?

~ 7 ~

BY FAITH: SORROWFUL, YET ALWAYS REJOICING

Observation & Interpretation

Habakkuk 3:16-19

Read Habakkuk 3:16-19 and consider the following questions.

 [16] I hear, and my body trembles;
   my lips quiver at the sound;
rottenness enters into my bones;
   my legs tremble beneath me.
Yet I will quietly wait for the day of trouble
   to come upon people who invade us.
   [17] Though the fig tree should not blossom,
   nor fruit be on the vines,
the produce of the olive fail
   and the fields yield no food,
the flock be cut off from the fold
   and there be no herd in the stalls,
[18] yet I will rejoice in the Lord;
   I will take joy in the God of my salvation.
[19] God, the Lord, is my strength;

he makes my feet like the deer's;
he makes me tread on my high places.
   To the choirmaster: with stringed instruments.

1. In verse 16, Habakkuk describes his deep emotion. What do you think he is responding to?

What does he resolve to do at the end of the verse?

2. Describe the conditions that Habakkuk details in verse 17.

3. Compare Habakkuk's prayers in 1:1-4 and 1:12-17 with his last prayer in 3:16-19. Describe the change that seems to have happened in Habakkuk's heart.

4. Consider verse 19 alongside **Psalm 18:31-36** as you ponder the imagery of the "feet of the deer's... treading on high places."

[31] For who is God, but the Lord?
   And who is a rock, except our God?—
[32] the God who equipped me with strength
   and made my way blameless.
[33] He made my feet like the feet of a deer
   and set me secure on the heights.
[34] He trains my hands for war,

so that my arms can bend a bow of bronze.
³⁵ You have given me the shield of your salvation,
 and your right hand supported me,
 and your gentleness made me great.
³⁶ You gave a wide place for my steps under me,
 and my feet did not slip.

What do you think Habakkuk is saying about the strength God gives?

Commentary & Conclusion

Habakkuk closes in prayer and gives us a beautiful picture of what it means to, amidst painful loss, have faith in God and receive life. He had taken refuge in the God who was acquainted with sorrow—and his prayer led him to trust and worship. We see in these last verses that even in the complex and taxing process of grief, the joy of salvation proves steadfast. Habakkuk does not minimize the suffering he foresees, but he shows us that as he, and all of God's people wait for God's rescue, we can grieve with hope. We can "take joy" in the God of our salvation.

Verse 16

First Habakkuk attempts to describe his reaction to God's words. He says, "I heard and my heart pounded, my lips quivered at the sound; decay crept into my bones, and my legs trembled." This is a deeply physical response to shock—Habakkuk's sincere pain and bewilderment are evident. His physical response might remind us of Jesus at Gethsemane, who also had a physical response to grief and fear when he experienced "agony" and "his sweat became like great drops of blood falling down to the ground" (Luke 22:44).

The next verses tell us what prompted Habakkuk's trembling fear. Habakkuk had considered and acknowledged the pain that they were about to face. He considered the loss ahead of him and felt all-consuming physical pain. "Yet", he resolved to "wait patiently for the day of calamity to come on the nation invading us."

The road to God's redemption would be costly, and Habakkuk felt the heavy weight of the judgement to come. But God had shown him His great saving strength; He promised to come "bring calamity" to Babylon and rescue Israel. Habakkuk would wait and hope by faith.

Verse 17

Habakkuk proves further that faith in God and acknowledgment of pain can happen at the same time. In verse 17, he considers the devastating consequences of what he is about to endure. In Habakkuk's life, wartime with Babylon would mean losing everything. He described in detail the effect it would have on agriculture, and some cultural context will help us understand the crushing effects this would have on the people. Robertson explains, "... the ravages of war shall leave the land desolate. The senseless rapacity of the invading army shall consume all that is worthwhile on the face of the earth. The consequent disruption of the basic structures of the family and other social orders shall eventuate in an unproductive land..." Each product on Habakkuk's list would have an impact on the people's survival. Fig, grapes, and olives are gifts and pleasures of the land, the grains fields, flock and cattle provide for more essential items like bread, milk, and meat. Without these products, Judah would be without items they desperately needed (Robertson, 1990, p. 245). Material goods, earthly possessions, and livelihood would fade and pass away before their eyes.

Verse 18

After acknowledging his suffering, his prayer is turned to worship as Habakkuk looks to God's anchoring character with the word "Yet." He says, "Yet, I will take joy in the Lord..." And as he shifts his gaze from his circumstances to God's promises, he chooses to use His covenant name, Yahweh. Habakkuk had appealed to God based on His covenant in the first cries of his prayer; he questioned how God's methods of judgement lined up with His promise to keep Israel. But Habakkuk's pouring out of his heart, and God's answer had changed him. He recalled God's record of steadfast love and faithfulness, and was led to trust His wise ways of working out salvation for His people. While Habakkuk's circumstances seemed uncertain, nothing eternal had changed. God restored Habakkuk's joy in His gracious promise of salvation.

Verse 19

The joy that comes with knowing and experiencing God gives His people strength. Habakkuk felt renewed strength as he reflected on God's secure promise. He illustrates his hopeful perspective by describing a deer- graceful, energetic, and light-footed even on the most treacherous of rocky heights. Though he knew grief was ahead—and grief is by no means tame or simple—he looked with confidence to the Savior who cared for him.

The last line of Habakkuk reads, "For the director of music. On my stringed instruments." Chapter 3 was a song not just for Habakkuk's personal faith and transformation, but for corporate lament and worship among God's people. This journey from grief to joy became a liturgy— a godly script for fellow sufferers. When the waiting was too weary and deep loss left them at a loss for words, Habakkuk's prayer would give them words to pour out that they might be guided in godly grief and godly praise.

More joy was coming for God's people. God was indeed faithful to His *everlasting covenant*, and He would save a remnant of this chosen nation **"by faith"** in Him. Jesus, "the lion of Judah," would *come* again as a descendent of Judah, as a Savior, and as a *glorious light* for those who walked in darkness. Jesus, the greater Habakkuk, would also grieve and cry out, "How long" over the injustice within Israel. And when He counted what the cost would be for justice and for His people's redemption, He poured out His heart to God in lament, and it caused Him deep trembling and physical agony. He remained faithful, grasping His grief in one hand while reaching for the joy set before Him with the other. His faith was in the God of Salvation and Resurrection. He was a victim of the layers of corrupt Israel as their leadership committed violent injustice on their Brother. And like Habakkuk, He experienced firsthand the devastating effects of a nation hungry for its own glory and drunk on power, and it *meant He would lose everything.* They nailed Him to a cross, and Jesus bore the judgment for the sin that He, and Habakkuk lamented. He was raised on the third day, demonstrating that *God is a Warrior of Salvation,* and *moves all nature and the cosmos* in order to rescue His people. He came so that our journey might be from *grief to eternal joy,* and lament to everlasting praise. Jesus bore the curse for us, and by faith in Him, God's everlasting covenant mercy and bless-ings would be and will be poured out on His people forever. If we live by faith in His life, death, and resurrection, we are given life, and an everlasting inheritance of joy and singing to the God of our Salvation.

Seeing Jesus Christ in Habakkuk

1. Consider statements about joy and satisfaction in **Philippians 3:7-11** and **Psalm 4:7-8** alongside Habakkuk 3:17-19. How does the joy of salvation in Christ give us strength during our suffering?

[7] But whatever gain I had, I counted as loss for the sake of Christ. [8] Indeed, I count everything as loss because of the surpassing worth of knowing Christ Jesus my Lord. For his sake I have suffered the loss of all things and count them as rubbish, in order that I may gain Christ [9] and be found in him, not having a righteousness of my own that comes from the law, but that which comes through faith in Christ, the righteousness from God that depends on faith— [10] that I may know him and the power of his resurrection, and may share his sufferings, becoming like him in his death, [11] that by any means possible I may attain the resurrection from the dead.

[7] You have put more joy in my heart
than they have when their grain and wine abound.
[8] In peace I will both lie down and sleep;
for you alone, O Lord, make me dwell in safety.

2. Read **2 Corinthians 4:7-12**, and **16-18**. Describe how Paul endures suffering while taking Joy in Jesus.

[7] But we have this treasure in jars of clay, to show that the surpassing power belongs to God and not to us. [8] We are afflicted in every way, but not crushed; perplexed, but not driven to despair; [9] persecuted, but not forsaken; struck down, but not destroyed; [10] always carrying in the body the death of Jesus, so that the life of Jesus may also be manifested in our bodies. [11] For we who live are always being given over to death for Jesus' sake, so that the life of Jesus also may be manifested in our mortal flesh. [12] So death is at work in us, but life in you.

[16] So we do not lose heart. Though our outer self is wasting away, our inner self is being renewed day by day. [17] For this light momentary affliction is preparing for us an eternal weight of glory beyond all comparison, [18] as we look not to the things that are seen but to the things that are unseen. For the things that are seen are transient, but the things that are unseen are eternal.

How do you think this is related to the call to live "by faith"?

3. Habakkuk grieved his losses and painful circumstances, "Yet," he rejoiced in the God of His Salvation. Sometimes we too face perplexing circumstances that seem to not line up with God's character. What does Christ's work at the cross tell us about God's:

Justice-

Love-

Mercy and Grace-

Sovereignty-

Describe how God's character displayed at the cross might offer us joy in tension with our painful trials.

Prayer & Journal Prompt

Take some time to thank and praise Jesus that He...

Proves Himself to be the source of everlasting eternal joy and all-surpassing peace in even the most painful circumstances.

Glorifies Himself as strength in our deepest weakness, and light through our brokenness and frailty.

Demonstrated the fullness of God's goodness and power by His work on the cross. So that when our feelings and circumstances waver, we might put our trust in the resurrection that came through the most tragic lament in history.

Showed us in the cross that God's perfect Justice, Love, Mercy, and Compassion have always been *for* us. And He works all things, even death, for the good of those who love Him.

Application & Reflection

1. Can you think of a time you experienced joy in Christ in tension with painful circumstances?

What did this event teach you about God?

2. How is grieving "yet taking joy" in Christ different from making light of our suffering or finding the "bright side" of pain?

What are some ways you desire to grow in Godly grief and Godly joy?

3. What have you learned from this study about Biblical Lament?

How might this perspective inform the way you walk alongside others as they suffer?

4. While he suffered, Habakkuk could "take joy" in the God of His Salvation. Read **Romans 8:28-39**.

[29] For those whom he foreknew he also predestined to be conformed to the image of his Son, in order that he might be the

firstborn among many brothers. [30] And those whom he predestined he also called, and those whom he called he also justified, and those whom he justified he also glorified.

[31] What then shall we say to these things? If God is for us, who can be against us? [32] He who did not spare his own Son but gave him up for us all, how will he not also with him graciously give us all things? [33] Who shall bring any charge against God's elect? It is God who justifies. [34] Who is to condemn? Christ Jesus is the one who died—more than that, who was raised—who is at the right hand of God, who indeed is interceding for us. [35] Who shall separate us from the love of Christ? Shall tribulation, or distress, or persecution, or famine, or nakedness, or danger, or sword? [36] As it is written,

"For your sake we are being killed all the day long;
we are regarded as sheep to be slaughtered."

[37] No, in all these things we are more than conquerors through him who loved us. [38] For I am sure that neither death nor life, nor angels nor rulers, nor things present nor things to come, nor powers, [39] nor height nor depth, nor anything else in all creation, will be able to separate us from the love of God in Christ Jesus our Lord.

What about the gospel offers unconditional joy?

5. What aspects of God's love and/or the gospel's unconditional joy might help you walk by faith as you consider your losses and endure trials this week?

BIBLIOGRAPHY

1. Citations marked "ESV Study Bible" are taken from the ESV® Study Bible (The Holy Bible, English Standard Version®), copyright ©2008 by Crossway, a publishing ministry of Good News Publishers. Used by permission. All rights reserved.

2. Scripture quotations are from the ESV® Bible (The Holy Bible, English Standard Version®), © 2001 by Crossway, a publishing ministry of Good News Publishers. Used by permission. All rights reserved. The ESV text may not be quoted in any publication made available to the public by a Creative Commons license. The ESV may not be translated in whole or in part into any other language. The Holy Bible, English Standard Version®, is adapted from the Revised Standard Version of the Bible, copyright Division of Christian Education of the National Council of the Churches of Christ in the U.S.A.

3. Scripture quotations marked (NIV) are taken from the Holy Bible, New International Version®, NIV®. Copyright © 1973, 1978, 1984, 2011 by Biblica, Inc.™ Used by permission of Zondervan. All rights reserved worldwide. www.zondervan.com The "NIV" and "New International Version" are trademarks registered in the United States Patent and Trademark Office by Biblica, Inc.™

4. Akin, Daniel. "Christocentric Hermeneutics." Hermeneutics, Southeastern Baptist Theological Seminary. Lecture handout.

5. Calvin, J., *Calvin's Commentaries Volume XV: Habakkuk, Zephaniah, Haggai, Zechariah, Malachi.* Grand Rapids, MI. Baker Books, a division of Baker Book House Company, Copyright 2005.

6. Redmond, Curtis, and Fentress, *Christ-Centered Exposition Commentary: Exalting Jesus in Jonah, Micah, Nahum, and Habakkuk.* Eric C Redmond, Bill Curtis, Ken Fentress. Nashville, Tennessee. B&H Publishing Group. Reprinted and used by permission. Copyright © 2016.

7. Robertson, O Palmer. *Eerdmans Classic Biblical Commentaries. The Books of Nahum, Habakkuk, and Zephaniah.* Grand Rapids, Michigan. Wm. B. Eerdmans Publishing Co. Copyright © 1990

8. Boice, James M. *The Minor Prophets: An Expositional Commentary.* Volume 2. Grand Rapids, Michigan. Baker Books. 1986.

9. Vroegop, Mark. *Dark Clouds, Deep Mercy: Discovering the Grace of Lament.* Wheaton, Illinois. Crossway, a publishing ministry of Good News Publishers. © 2019 Mark Vroegop.

www.ingramcontent.com/pod-product-compliance
Lightning Source LLC
Chambersburg PA
CBHW070725130626
46553CB00005B/2153